467 0456

363.728 Stefoff, Rebecca,
STE   1951-

        Recycling. BRANCH

$19.95

RECYCLING

EARTH ● AT ● RISK

Acid Rain

Alternative Sources of Energy

Animal Welfare

The Automobile and the Environment

Clean Air

Clean Water

Degradation of the Land

Economics of Environmental Protection

Environmental Action Groups

The Environment and the Law

Environmental Disasters

Extinction

The Fragile Earth

Global Warming

The Living Ocean

Nuclear Energy/Nuclear Waste

Overpopulation

The Ozone Layer

Recycling

The Rain Forest

Solar Energy

Toxic Materials

What You Can Do for the Environment

RECYCLING

by Rebecca Stefoff

Introduction by
Russell E. Train

Chairman of
the Board of Directors,
World Wildlife Fund and
The Conservation Foundation

CHELSEA HOUSE PUBLISHERS

new york   philadelphia

CHELSEA HOUSE PUBLISHERS
EDITOR-IN-CHIEF: Remmel Nunn
MANAGING EDITOR: Karyn Gullen Browne
COPY CHIEF: Juliann Barbato
PICTURE EDITOR: Adrian G. Allen
ART DIRECTOR: Maria Epes
DEPUTY COPY CHIEF: Mark Rifkin
ASSISTANT ART DIRECTOR: Noreen Romano
MANUFACTURING MANAGER: Gerald Levine
SYSTEMS MANAGER: Lindsey Ottman
PRODUCTION MANAGER: Joseph Romano
PRODUCTION COORDINATOR: Marie Claire Cebrián

EARTH AT RISK
Senior Editor: Jake Goldberg

Staff for *Recycling*
COPY EDITOR: Brian Sookram
EDITORIAL ASSISTANT: Ian Wilker
PICTURE RESEARCHER: Sandy Jones
DESIGNER: Maria Epes
LAYOUT: Marjorie Zaum

 This book is printed on recycled paper.

3 5 7 9 8 6 4 2

Library of Congress Cataloging-in-Publication Data
Stefoff, Rebecca
  Recycling/Rebecca Stefoff; introduction by Russell Train.
    p. cm.—(Earth at risk)
  Includes index.
  Summary: Examines the evolution of recycling as a concept, its
role in controlling the world's trash problems, and possible future
developments.
  ISBN 0-7910-1573-4
      0-7910-1598-X (pbk.)
  1. Recycling (Waste, etc.)—Juvenile literature. 2. Waste
minimization—Juvenile literature. [1. Recycling (Waste) 2.
Refuse and refuse disposal.] I. Title. II. Series.   90-47039
TD794.5.S735 1991   CIP
363.72'82—dc20   AC

C O N T E N T S

Introduction—Russell E. Train   6

1   Trashing the World   13

2   The Recycling Alternative   27

3   Paper and Organic Waste   41

4   Glass and Metal   57

5   Plastics   69

6   Does Recycling Make a Difference?   81

7   Taming the Waste Stream   93

8   Toward a Reusable World   101

    Appendix: For More Information   116

    Further Reading   118

    Glossary   121

    Index   124

INTRODUCTION

Russell E. Train

Administrator, Environmental Protection Agency, 1973 to 1977; Chairman of the Board of Directors, World Wildlife Fund and The Conservation Foundation

There is a growing realization that human activities increasingly are threatening the health of the natural systems that make life possible on this planet. Humankind has the power to alter nature fundamentally, perhaps irreversibly.

This stark reality was dramatized in January 1989 when *Time* magazine named Earth the "Planet of the Year." In the same year, the Exxon *Valdez* disaster sparked public concern over the effects of human activity on vulnerable ecosystems when a thick blanket of crude oil coated the shores and wildlife of Prince William Sound in Alaska. And, no doubt, the 20th anniversary celebration of Earth Day in April 1990 renewed broad public interest in environmental issues still further. It is no accident then that many people are calling the years between 1990 and 2000 the "Decade of the Environment."

And this is not merely a case of media hype, for the 1990s will truly be a time when the people of the planet Earth learn the meaning of the phrase "everything is connected to everything else" in the natural and man-made systems that sustain our lives. This will be a period when more people will understand that burning a tree in Amazonia adversely affects the global atmosphere just as much as the exhaust from the cars that fill our streets and expressways.

Central to our understanding of environmental issues is the need to recognize the complexity of the problems we face and the relationships between environmental and other needs in our society. Global warming provides an instructive example. Controlling emissions of carbon dioxide, the principal greenhouse gas, will involve efforts to reduce the use of fossil fuels to generate electricity. Such a reduction will include energy conservation and the promotion of alternative energy sources, such as nuclear and solar power.

The automobile contributes significantly to the problem. We have the choice of switching to more energy efficient autos and, in the longer run, of choosing alternative automotive power systems and relying more on mass transit. This will require different patterns of land use and development, patterns that are less transportation and energy intensive.

In agriculture, rice paddies and cattle are major sources of greenhouse gases. Recent experiments suggest that universally used nitrogen fertilizers may inhibit the ability of natural soil organisms to take up methane, thus contributing tremendously to the atmospheric loading of that gas—one of the major culprits in the global warming scenario.

As one explores the various parameters of today's pressing environmental challenges, it is possible to identify some areas where we have made some progress. We have taken important steps to control gross pollution over the past two decades. What I find particularly encouraging is the growing environmental consciousness and activism by today's youth. In many communities across the country, young people are working together to take their environmental awareness out of the classroom and apply it to everyday problems. Successful recycling and tree-planting projects have been launched as a result of these budding environmentalists who have committed themselves to a cleaner environment. Citizen action, activated by youthful enthusiasm, was largely responsible for the fast-food industry's switch from rain forest to domestic beef, for pledges from important companies in the tuna industry to use fishing techniques that would not harm dolphins, and the recent announcement by the McDonald's Corporation to phase out polystyrene "clam shell" hamburger containers.

Despite these successes, much remains to be done if we are to make ours a truly healthy environment. Even a short list of persistent issues includes problems such as acid rain, ground-level ozone and

smog, and airborne toxins; ground water protection and nonpoint
sources of pollution such as runoff from farms and city streets; wetlands
protection; hazardous waste dumps; and solid waste disposal, waste
minimization, and recycling.

Similarly, there is an unfinished agenda in the natural resources
area: effective implementation of newly adopted management plans for
national forests; strengthening the wildlife refuge system; national park
management, including addressing the growing pressure of development
on lands surrounding the parks; implementation of the Endangered
Species Act; wildlife trade problems, such as that involving elephant
ivory; and ensuring adequate sustained funding for these efforts at all
levels of government. All of these issues are before us today; most will
continue in one form or another through the year 2000.

Each of these challenges to environmental quality and our
health requires a response that recognizes the complex nature of the
problem. Narrowly conceived solutions will not achieve lasting results.
Often it seems that when we grab hold of one part of the environmental
balloon, an unsightly and threatening bulge appears somewhere else.

The higher environmental issues arise on the national agenda,
the more important it is that we are armed with the best possible
knowledge of the economic costs of undertaking particular environmental programs and the costs associated with not undertaking them.
Our society is not blessed with unlimited resources, and tough choices
are going to have to be made. These should be informed choices.

All too often, environmental objectives are seen as at cross
purposes with other considerations vital to our society. Thus,
environmental protection is often viewed as being in conflict with
economic growth, with energy needs, with agricultural productions, and
so on. The time has come when environmental considerations must be
fully integrated into every nation's priorities.

One area that merits full legislative attention is energy
efficiency. The United States is one of the least energy efficient of all the
industrialized nations. Japan, for example, uses far less energy per unit of
gross national product than the United States does. Of course, a country
as large as the United States requires large amounts of energy for
transportation. However, there is still a substantial amount of excess
energy used, and this excess constitutes waste. More fuel efficient autos

and home heating systems would save millions of barrels of oil, or their equivalent, each year. And air pollutants, including greenhouse gases, could be significantly reduced by increased efficiency in industry.

I suspect that the environmental problem that comes closest to home for most of us is the problem of what to do with trash. All over the world, communities are wrestling with the problem of waste disposal. Landfill sites are rapidly filling to capacity. No one wants a trash and garbage dump near home. As William Ruckelshaus, former EPA administrator and now in the waste management business, puts it, "Everyone wants you to pick up the garbage and no one wants you to put it down!"

At the present time, solid waste programs emphasize the regulation of disposal, setting standards for landfills and so forth. In the decade ahead, we must shift our emphasis from regulating waste disposal to an overall reduction in its volume. We must look at the entire waste stream, including product design and packaging. We must avoid creating waste in the first place. To the greatest extent possible, we should then recycle any waste that is produced. I believe that, while most of us enjoy our comfortable way of life and have no desire to change things, we also know in our hearts that our "disposable society" has allowed us to become pretty soft.

Land use is another domestic issue that might well attract legislative attention by the year 2000. All across the United States, communities are grappling with the problem of growth. All too often, growth imposes high costs on the environment—the pollution of aquifers; the destruction of wetlands; the crowding of shorelines; the loss of wildlife habitat; and the loss of those special places, such as a historic structure or area, that give a community a sense of identity. It is worth noting that growth is not only the product of economic development but of population movement. By the year 2010, for example, experts predict that 75% of all Americans will live within 50 miles of a coast.

It is important to keep in mind that we are all made vulnerable by environmental problems that cross international borders. Of course, the most critical global conservation problems are the destruction of tropical forests and the consequent loss of their biological capital. Some scientists have calculated extinction rates as high as 11 species per hour. All agree that the loss of species has never been greater than at the present time; not even the disappearance of the dinosaurs can compare to today's rate of extinction.

In addition to species extinctions, the loss of tropical forests may represent as much as 20% of the total carbon dioxide loadings to the atmosphere. Clearly, any international approach to the problem of global warming must include major efforts to stop the destruction of forests and to manage those that remain on a renewable basis. Debt for nature swaps, which the World Wildlife Fund has pioneered in Costa Rica, Ecuador, Madagascar, and the Philippines, provide a useful mechanism for promoting such conservation objectives.

Global environmental issues inevitably will become the principal focus in international relations. But the single overriding issue facing the world community today is how to achieve a sustainable balance between growing human populations and the earth's natural systems. If you travel as frequently as I do in the developing countries of Latin America, Africa, and Asia, it is hard to escape the reality that expanding human populations are seriously weakening the earth's resource base. Rampant deforestation, eroding soils, spreading deserts, loss of biological diversity, the destruction of fisheries, and polluted and degraded urban environments threaten to spread environmental impoverishment, particularly in the tropics where human population growth is greatest.

It is important to recognize that environmental degradation and human poverty are closely linked. Impoverished people desperate for land on which to grow crops or graze cattle are destroying forests and overgrazing even more marginal land. These people become trapped in a vicious downward spiral. They have little choice but to continue to overexploit the weakened resources available to them. Continued abuse of these lands only diminishes their productivity. Throughout the developing world, alarming amounts of land rendered useless by overgrazing and poor agricultural practices have become virtual wastelands, yet human numbers continue to multiply in these areas.

From Bangladesh to Haiti, we are confronted with an increasing number of ecological basket cases. In the Philippines, a traditional focus of U.S. interest, environmental devastation is widespread as deforestation, soil erosion, and the destruction of coral reefs and fisheries combine with the highest population growth rate in Southeast Asia.

Controlling human population growth is the key factor in the environmental equation. World population is expected to at least double to about 11 billion before leveling off. Most of this growth will occur in the poorest nations of the developing world. I would hope that the United States will once again become a strong advocate of international efforts to promote family planning. Bringing human populations into a sustainable balance with their natural resource base must be a vital objective of U.S. foreign policy.

Foreign economic assistance, the program of the Agency for International Development (AID), can become a potentially powerful tool for arresting environmental deterioration in developing countries. People who profess to care about global environmental problems—the loss of biological diversity, the destruction of tropical forests, the greenhouse effect, the impoverishment of the marine environment, and so on—should be strong supporters of foreign aid planning and the principles of sustainable development urged by the World Commission on Environment and Development, the "Brundtland Commission."

If sustainability is to be the underlying element of overseas assistance programs, so too must it be a guiding principle in people's practices at home. Too often we think of sustainable development only in terms of the resources of other countries. We have much that we can and should be doing to promote long-term sustainability in our own resource management. The conflict over our own rain forests, the old growth forests of the Pacific Northwest, illustrates this point.

The decade ahead will be a time of great activity on the environmental front, both globally and domestically. I sincerely believe we will be tested as we have been only in times of war and during the Great Depression. We must set goals for the year 2000 that will challenge both the American people and the world community.

Despite the complexities ahead, I remain an optimist. I am confident that if we collectively commit ourselves to a clean, healthy environment we can surpass the achievements of the 1980s and meet the serious challenges that face us in the coming decades. I hope that today's students will recognize their significant role in and responsibility for bringing about change and will rise to the occasion to improve the quality of our global environment.

A garbage dump in Cairo, Egypt. This family actually lives in the dump and makes its living collecting garbage. The problem of trash disposal is a worldwide one.

c h a p t e r   1

T R A S H I N G   T H E   W O R L D

On the outskirts of Manila, the capital of the Philippines, rises a big, sprawling hill. It is called Smokey Mountain because of the dull haze of smoke that constantly drifts skyward from its smoldering depths. But Smokey Mountain is not a volcano—it is a trash dump the size of a town. It grows bigger every day, and it even has inhabitants: 20,000 dump dwellers who live in shacks made of trash and who pick through Smokey Mountain's steaming mounds of garbage and its suburbs of rubbish in search of something they can eat or sell for a few cents.

Smokey Mountain is an impressively large pile of waste, but it is insignificant next to a monument that is being built in Staten Island, New York. This monument covers an area of 3,000 acres. When it is completed in the late 1990s, it will reach a height of more than 500 feet and will be larger than the Great Pyramid of Egypt. In fact, it will be the highest point on the Atlantic seacoast of the United States from Florida to Maine, and it will rival the Great Wall of China as the world's largest man-made artifact. This mammoth construction is the Fresh Kills landfill, the biggest trash dump in the world, where more than 18,000 tons of New York City's garbage are deposited daily. In early 1990, Fresh Kills was estimated to hold more than 100 million tons of trash and garbage, some of it dating back to the late 1940s. Each day, the landfill leaks more than a million gallons of toxic leachate—a poisonous soup that is brewed when rain absorbs chemicals from rust, paint, batteries, and other hazardous trash—into local waterways.

Besides possessing the world's largest trash dump, Americans lead the world in trash and garbage production. Among industrialized peoples, the average Japanese throws away 2.2 pounds of trash each day; the average German, 2.5 pounds; and the average American, 3.5 pounds. Each year, Americans throw away a total of 18 billion disposable diapers, 220 million automobile tires, 1.6 billion disposable plastic pens, 2 billion disposable razors and blades, more than 11 million tons of plastic soda and milk bottles, enough aluminum to rebuild all the airplanes of all the commercial U.S. airlines 4 times over, enough paper and wood to heat 5 million homes for 200 years, and enough television sets to reach from New York City to Denver—about 7.6 million of them. American homes produce a total of 160 million tons of trash annually. American businesses add another 70 million tons; American farms, mines, and factories produce 5 billion tons of solid waste each year.

The American way with trash is influencing other parts of the globe as well. The products of a "disposable" society are seen in the rubbish that litters once-pristine places of the world. Mount Everest, the world's highest peak, is the most inaccessible place on earth, yet even here the refuse discarded by climbing expeditions over the years has created the world's highest garbage dump—at 18,000 feet above sea level on the south side of the mountain. By 1987, Mount Everest had been so badly trashed that

The remotest parts of the earth are not safe from the trash crisis. Here, garbage left by climbing expeditions litters the approaches to Mount Everest in the Himalayas.

a special expedition was sent up the mountain just to clean up the mess left behind by previous climbers.

PEOPLE AND GARBAGE

Garbage is as old as human society. Modern archaeologists and anthropologists eagerly excavate middens, or pits where trash and refuse were dumped, for clues about the diets and habits of the earliest human ancestors. For thousands of years, people lived in small groups, and each little community could dispose of its biological wastes, bones and skins, fire ash, and broken stone tools without much trouble. But as societies grew larger and more sophisticated, so did their waste disposal problems. The earliest recorded municipal garbage rules were published in Athens, Greece, around 500 B.C.—citizens were asked to dump their refuse a mile or more outside the city limits. Throughout most of Europe, however, people were less fastidious; residents of Paris, London, and other cities disposed of their garbage by hurling it out their windows into the streets and gutters until well into the 19th century.

In the United States, most communities had organized waste disposal services by the early years of the 20th century. Trash and garbage were generally burned, although pickers, or scavengers, were employed to examine the refuse before it went into the fire and to remove anything that was reusable or could be

A member of the trash pickers "union," this Mexico City woman has scoured the city's massive dumps for usable materials for resale.

sold. Similar practices are common around the world today. In both India and Egypt, for example, whole castes of families make their living by collecting, sorting, and marketing trash. In Mexico City, access to the city's trash dumps—where up to 20,000 tons of trash are unloaded each day—is limited to scavengers who have joined the trash pickers' "union" and paid fees to the dump guards.

World War II (1939–45) greatly affected American attitudes toward garbage. International trade was disrupted, yet the nation's factories had to churn out tanks, planes, and munitions in large quantities. Raw materials were at a premium. Conserving tin cans, scrap metal, glass, paper, and even nylon stockings became a patriotic duty, so that these materials could be recycled for the war effort. Industries in the United States recycled about 25% of the country's solid waste during the war years. But the boom in industrial expansion that followed the war started a spiral of manufacturing, consuming, and discarding that has continued into the 1990s. For decades the United States and other industrialized nations have been producing more garbage per person annually, but every year the number of places to put the trash gets smaller.

Much of the blame for the world's current trash disposal problem must fall on what environmental activists call "the throwaway life-style" or "the disposable society." Manufacturers and advertisers have learned that consumers place a high value on convenience and disposability. Today, many products—such as cans, bottles, paper napkins, and even paper clothing—are designed and manufactured to be used once and then thrown away. Other consumer goods, ranging from wristwatches and umbrellas all the way to major appliances such as air conditioners

During World War II, when war materials were in short supply, recycling became patriotic. Here, Boy Scouts in San Francisco collect aluminum pots and pans.

and VCRs, are manufactured in such a way that it is often cheaper and easier to discard and replace them if they break down than it is to have them repaired. A study cited in *Saving the Earth: A Citizen's Guide to Environmental Action* showed that 26% of the solid waste that is thrown away in the United States consists of items that are *designed* to be discarded: disposable diapers, throwaway plastic pens and watches, and the like. Another 34% of America's trash consists of packaging: the paper, plastic film, cardboard, and Styrofoam that swathes most mail and purchases, often in two or more layers.

The Environmental Protection Agency (EPA) classifies U.S. trash this way: 41% is paper (the bulk of it newspapers); 18% is organic yard waste (mown grass and raked leaves); 9% is metal; 8% is glass; 8% is organic food waste; 7% is plastic; and 9% belongs to other categories (medical and chemical waste, rubber, wood, and textiles, for example). As for volume, the EPA says that America's "Gross Garbage Product" each year would fill a convoy of garbage trucks 145,000 miles long—in other words, one that would reach more than halfway to the moon.

What happens to all of this trash? As of 1990, the United States buried 80% of its refuse in large underground dumps called landfills, burned 10% of it in special furnaces called incinerators, and recycled 10% of it. But more and more people are claiming that these percentages must change, and soon.

BURY IT OR BURN IT?

Until the 1970s, landfills seemed to most people to be the perfect solution to trash disposal headaches. There appeared to be an endless supply of out-of-the-way places to put trash. Today, however, population pressures and land costs are putting the squeeze on the landfill business. But the most serious drawback to landfills is the dangerous waste that oozes out of them. Most garbage contains moisture, and when that moisture is compressed in a landfill and then increased by rainfall, it leaches, or penetrates, into the surrounding ground, carrying with it hazardous chemicals and bacteria absorbed from the garbage. Furthermore, the process of decomposition, or organic decay, that takes place inside landfills produces methane, a gas that can leak into nearby soil, where it kills plant life, and into the air, where it produces an unpleasant odor and can be carried into neighboring buildings and woodlands.

In 1984, there were 9,000 landfills in use in the United States. By early 1990, that number had shrunk to about 6,000. Some 3,000 landfills were closed in less than 6 years, either because they were full to the limit or because the EPA determined that they posed an environmental hazard. EPA experts estimate that another 2,000 American landfills will be filled to capacity and closed down by 1993. In the meantime, it has become almost impossible to open new landfills for two reasons: First, government regulations for landfill operators are both complex and expensive to follow. Second, community resistance has ruled out many proposed landfill sites; this is called the NIMBY syndrome (for "not in *my* back yard"). As a result, U.S. communities are having to send their trash farther and farther afield to be dumped. Philadelphia has no landfill of its own and must pay landfills in Maryland, Virginia, and Ohio at least $44 million each year to take its trash, and New Jersey, which has the nation's worst trash disposal crisis, is forced to dump its garbage as far away as New Mexico.

During the 1970s, incineration appeared to offer bright prospects for trash disposal. By turning trash and garbage into ash, incineration can reduce the volume of solid waste by as much as 90%. It can also produce energy in the form of steam or electricity that can be fed into the community's utilities system. This "trash-to-steam" or "garbage-to-gold" aspect of incineration appeals to many people who are concerned about saving money and conserving energy.

But incineration plants are extremely expensive to build and operate, and studies during the 1980s showed that they often fail to meet federal or state air pollution standards. Environmentalists' biggest objection to incinerators, however, is that burning the trash produces harmful by-products: heat, air pollution, and ash.

The heat generated by trash combustion, when not efficiently channeled into an energy-producing system, can have a damaging effect on local water and wildlife. The air that is emitted from incinerators often contains acid gases, such as sulfur dioxide and hydrochloric acid, which contribute to acid rain, and carbon monoxide and hydrocarbons, which contribute to smog. Incinerators are equipped with devices called scrubbers that are supposed to remove harmful substances from the discharged air, but the effectiveness of these scrubbers varies widely and remains

Incinerating garbage reduces its bulk but still generates waste products, some of which can be toxic. Bottom ash from burned trash piles up next to this incinerator plant in Philadelphia.

The infamous garbage barge Mobro 4000, *carrying 3,000 tons of garbage from Long Island, New York, that nobody wanted to accept for disposal. The* Mobro *is here seen in the Gulf of Mexico off the Louisiana coast, more than a thousand miles from its cargo's point of origin.*

open to dispute. Finally, the ash that is left in incinerators after trash is burned poses a disposal problem in itself. About 90% of this ash is a relatively harmless and useless material called bottom ash. The other 10% is fly ash, which consists of very fine particles that can enter the air. Fly ash often contains hazardous or even poisonous metals and chemical compounds that are not destroyed in the burning process. When the fly ash is deposited in landfills, these chemicals can leach into the soil and the groundwater. Fearful of the dangers that may be posed by toxic air emissions and ash, environmental groups have persuaded voters and political leaders in many communities to halt the planned construction of new incinerators or to shut down existing ones.

NEXT TIME. . .TRY RECYCLING

The saga of the *Mobro 4000* illustrates the dilemma of a world wallowing in trash, with nowhere to put it. The *Mobro* was a garbage barge that was loaded in 1987 with 3,186 tons of refuse from an overflowing landfill in the town of Islip, on Long Island, New York. For 164 days, the *Mobro* cruised the Atlantic coast and the Gulf of Mexico, looking for a place that would let it unload its cargo of trash. Ports in North Carolina, Florida, Alabama, Mississippi, and Louisiana rejected it. The owners of the barge then attempted to land at foreign ports, only to be turned away in the Bahamas, Mexico, and Belize. The "Islip garbage barge," as it was called in the media, became famous. Talk show hosts surveyed it from helicopters, and its woeful progress was reported in daily newscasts. At first the plight of the barge was regarded as a joke; then it became an embarrassment. Finally it was seen as a symbol of some pressing questions that needed to be answered not just by Islip but by the entire global community: What can be done with garbage? And why is there so much of it?

Eventually, after covering more than 6,000 miles in its luckless search for a dump, the *Mobro* returned to the New York City area, still laden with its original cargo. The barge spent three

A local troop of Boy Scouts catches the recycling fever. Collecting and bagging metal cans means extra income for these environmentally conscious youngsters.

months in the harbor while municipal officials and trash disposal experts argued over its fate, until finally the cargo was burned in an incinerator in Brooklyn. The 400 tons of ash that remained were shipped back to Islip, to be buried in the same landfill that had originally sent the *Mobro* out to sea.

The story of the *Mobro* illustrates the growing dilemma of trash disposal, but perhaps it also contains a hint of hope for the future. During the barge's final sojourn off the shores of New York

City, activists from the environmental group Greenpeace took the opportunity to suggest one answer to the troubling questions that had been raised in the course of the *Mobro*'s voyage. They draped its bow with a huge and much-publicized banner that read Next Time . . . Try Recycling. And one year after burying the ash from the *Mobro*'s cargo in its landfill, the town of Islip introduced a model waste disposal program in which citizens are required by law to separate glass, paper, and metal from their trash so that these materials can be recycled. By 1990 the recycling program had tripled the volume of recyclable materials collected in Islip at an average savings of $2 million a year. The program had also added a few years to the projected life span of the Islip landfill. For Islip and the world, recycling is clearly not the whole solution to the debris dilemma, but it is an important part of the solution.

On Earth Day, 1990, spectators juggle a beach ball resembling the earth. Both protest and celebration, the annual Earth Day festival, with gatherings all over the country, has made many individuals conscious of the need for recycling.

chapter 2

THE RECYCLING
ALTERNATIVE

If both burying trash and burning it involve serious drawbacks, what can be done with it? The Greenpeace "environmental guerrillas" who draped their banner across the *Mobro* barge reminded the world of one solution: recycling. They called attention to the fact that the barge's load of festering garbage would not have existed—or would have been much smaller—if the society that turned its discards into trash had recycled those discards instead. Recycling is a method of trash disposal that is practiced by a growing number of individuals, communities, and nations around the world.

The key to understanding what recycling is and how it works lies in the word itself. It is based on *cycle*, which comes from the Greek word *kyklos*, which means "circle," or "wheel." A cycle is simply a series of events or processes that returns to its starting point over and over again, as a bicycle wheel spins around and around. One example of a cyclical process is the cycle of the seasons, which repeat themselves with endless, unvarying regularity as the earth moves in a great circle around the sun.

The processes that sustain life on the planet are sometimes referred to as the cycle of nature. Living things are nourished by what they take from the environment: Plants consume water and soil nutrients along with carbon dioxide from the atmosphere, and animals consume plants and other animals and breathe oxygen. The wastes that all living things excrete are consumed by tiny microorganisms. In the process of consuming, microorganisms break wastes down into their component elements and return them to the environment. The same thing happens to dead plants and animals. The material that is released into the environment from decaying plants and animals supports new generations of plants and animals.

Life thus exists within a cycle in which matter is produced, consumed, and reused. The energy that drives the entire cycle comes from sunlight, which is captured by the chlorophyll pigment in green plants and transformed into plant growth. "The natural world is built on throwaway parts," points out biologist George Hendry in an article in the May 1990 issue of *Natural History* magazine. But Hendry adds that there is an important difference between nature's throwaway world and mankind's consumer-oriented society: "Natural products are biodegradable," that is, they can be broken down, or degraded, into their component elements by biological processes and then reabsorbed into the environment.

For many thousands of years, human beings—like all of the other animal species on the planet—lived within this natural biological cycle of growth, decay, and renewal. They consumed plants and animals and produced only what could be absorbed by the environment. If the place in which they lived became too cluttered with food waste, excrement, and fire ash to be comfortable, they simply moved on to a new place and left the old habitat to be cleansed over time by wind, rain, fire, and microorganisms.

THE BROKEN CYCLE

In the past few millennia, the human species has stepped outside the cycle of nature. People have settled in larger and still larger communities, until today millions live in megalopolises such as Tokyo, New York City, and Mexico City—cities that cannot be picked up and relocated when the land and water get dirty. Humans have also developed medical skills that save lives and alleviate suffering, but in doing so they have increased their numbers and prolonged their life spans. In 1990, there were more

More than 100 years ago, the famous satirical cartoonist Thomas Nast attacked the problem of pollution in New York City.

than 5 billion people in the world, up from about 5 million in 8000 B.C. That is an increase of more than 100,000% in only 10,000 years—a very short period of time compared to the long eons over which the earth's natural balances were worked out and sustained.

Ever since the beginning of the Industrial Revolution in England in the late 18th century, people have shifted natural resources around the planet in great quantities and introduced new processes—such as the large-scale combustion of fossil fuels in automobile engines, factories, and power plants—that have overloaded the environment's ability to absorb waste. People have begun producing large quantities of goods other than those needed to provide food, clothing, and shelter—often, more goods than can be consumed. Finally, and perhaps most importantly from the point of view of trash disposal, people have created new materials by combining natural substances in new ways through industrial processes. These materials are called man-made because they do not exist in nature, although the raw materials for making them occur naturally. And because these substances do not occur in nature, they cannot easily be absorbed and reused by the physical environment. Chief among these man-made substances are the more than 45 varieties of plastic and the chemical compounds produced as by-products of industrial processes and combustion.

The natural cycle of renewal has snapped under these pressures. Human beings must now cope with the inevitable result of breaking the cycle. They are creating waste in unprecedented quantities and also in new, man-made forms—and all of this waste, instead of being absorbed by the environment, just stays around. It accumulates. This means that matter is constantly taken out of the planetwide cycle of decay and reuse. It also means that the human race has a big trash disposal problem on its hands, and the problem is getting bigger every day.

The concept of recycling is based on nature's cycle of reuse. Broadly speaking, recycling is any activity that keeps matter in use. Just as biological processes recycle dead plants and animals and the waste products of living ones by turning them into food, energy, and new life, human recyclers try to keep all sorts of human waste within a cycle of use and reuse. Their methods can be divided into three general categories:

1.   Integrating waste back into the cycle of nature. This includes using excrement as fertilizer and composting food waste and lawn clippings to make garden soil.

2.   Using materials more than once for the same or similar purposes. This includes using refillable glass bottles instead of disposable plastic ones for spring water, printing newspapers on paper made from old newspapers that have been shredded and processed into recycled paper, and making new aluminum beverage cans out of used ones rather than out of raw materials.

3.   Finding new ways to use materials that would otherwise be discarded. An individual might do this by using a glass jar that originally contained spaghetti sauce to hold pens and pencils instead of throwing it in the trash. On a larger scale, corporations are developing ways to break down plastic soda bottles and remake them into different products, such as park benches and fence posts.

Garbage is not simply an American problem; trash disposal has become a major headache for cities such as Shanghai. The largest city in China, Shanghai is plagued by overpopulation as well as traffic congestion.

These activities, and many more, are included in the overall process of recycling. The raw material of recycling is what environmentalists call the waste stream, which is the total amount of waste produced by any community—from a household to a nation. The waste streams of factories and power plants include industrial by-products, ash, and particles emitted from smokestacks. The waste streams of large office buildings include enormous amounts of discarded paper, typewriter ribbon cartridges, and similar materials. Each person's individual waste stream consists of everything that he or she throws into a wastebasket or trash can, grinds up in a garbage disposal, thoughtlessly litters on the street, throws from a car window, leaves uneaten on a restaurant plate, or flushes down the toilet. In the United States and nearly all industrialized or urban settings around the world, sewage waste is generally disposed of by government agencies, so the typical individual does not have very much control over that part of his or her waste stream. The other parts of each person's individual waste stream, however, are subject to a great deal of control. And groups of people, from neighborhoods to international associations, can determine how the communal waste stream will be handled.

Various terms have been used to refer to the components of the waste stream. Traditionally, the word *garbage* has been used to refer primarily to food wastes, or the sort of waste that could be put into a kitchen sink garbage disposal. *Trash* has been used to refer to other kinds of waste: paper, cans and bottles, cardboard boxes, and junk in general. Another word that was once widely used to describe waste is *rubbish.* This term is less common today, but when it is used it generally refers to trash, and particularly to useless or discarded objects such as old appliances and clothing, rather than to food or organic waste. The distinction between garbage and trash has become blurred in recent years because most waste collection and waste disposal facilities mix all kinds of waste together. Nearly all landfills, for example, contain pork chop bones and grapefruit rinds right on top of old newspapers and broken typewriters; and many incinerators are of the type called mass burn facilities, which means that they burn waste without sorting it. As a result, today most environmentalists and waste disposal workers use *garbage* and *trash* interchangeably to refer to everything in the waste stream except sewage and air emissions. Another term that is gaining general acceptance is *solid waste*, which distinguishes garbage or trash from the liquid or airborne parts of the waste stream. Individual waste items are collected from households and businesses by private haulers or municipal services, piled by the truckload in dumps, and eventually disposed of in landfills or incinerators. These masses of gathered garbage are called MSWs, or *municipal solid wastes.*

FROM FLOWER POWER TO PUBLIC POLICY

Recycling has a long history. Until perhaps a century or so ago, most people and communities practiced what is now called recycling without giving it a second thought. Waste was rare. Worn-out clothing became rags; food waste was fed to farm animals or thrown out where nature could absorb it; glass containers were reused over and over; waste paper was saved to start fires, to stuff mattresses, or to be used as toilet paper; and broken objects of wood or metal were repaired or taken apart so that their materials could be used in other items. These were routine practices for all except perhaps the very rich, and even their discarded trash was usually gathered and reused in some way by the poor. Life still follows this pattern in parts of the world that have had little exposure to Western-style industrialization and mass-produced man-made materials, but such places are increasingly rare.

The impossibility of depending upon landfills to solve the garbage problem is dramatically illustrated in this photograph of a tractor trying to maneuver through the trash overflow.

Although the late 19th and early 20th centuries brought sudden increases in city populations and in the volume of manufactured goods, trash still seemed manageable. Communities realized that they could no longer continue to rid themselves of their waste in a casual manner, by simply tossing it into a corner of their property or carting it to the town dump. Instead, individual families and farms and then whole towns began to burn their waste. According to the authors of *Saving the Earth: A Citizen's Guide to Environmental Action,* the organized incineration of collected trash began in Nottingham, England, in 1874. This was the forerunner of today's multimillion-dollar HTRRs, or high-technology resource recovery units, as state-of-the-art incinerators are called. Within a few decades, mass incinerators had been built in many communities worldwide, and by 1913 the burning of trash was producing electricity at a pioneer trash-to-steam plant in Milwaukee, Wisconsin.

Trash was being burned in large quantities, but it was almost always sorted first, either by homeowners or municipal employees. Scrap metal was the first part of the waste stream to be separated; it was eagerly sought by scrap metal dealers, who circulated through towns and neighborhoods in horse-drawn carts, and later in trucks, buying old metal goods for a few cents per pound. These dealers later sold the scrap to manufacturers of sheet or cast metal, who used it as a raw material, melting it down to make new products. Wood, paper, and glass were also routinely separated from trash and were often resold to dealers, eventually to be reused in manufacturing.

World War II gave the world's factories an insatiable hunger for raw materials and thus intensified the recovery of resources from waste throughout the industrialized world. The years after the war, however, brought a boom in international trade, in manufacturing of all kinds, and in population. They also brought a change in how trash was handled. After the chronic shortages of the war years, materials and products of all sorts seemed abundant. Consumers were eagerly attracted to items that promised convenience, so disposable goods were born. More and more products were designed, produced, and bought for what environmentalist Cynthia Pollock of the Worldwatch Institute has called a "one-night stand"—an easy one-time use followed by a descent into the waste stream. To many people, the idea of sorting and hoarding trash seemed like an outworn relic of a dour past. Not only did most individuals and families stop sorting their waste and conserving part of it, but municipal waste disposal programs eliminated the sorting step as well.

This friendly looking trash "igloo" is designed to encourage young people to recycle their waste. In use, it would be labeled with the kind of material to be recycled—glass, metal, plastic, and so on.

At the same time, the highly visible ash and smoke from incinerators began to cause concern. By the 1960s, many incinerators had been shut down because they were inefficient to operate and caused too much air pollution to be ignored. Landfills, in which garbage and trash of all sorts could be dumped indiscriminately and then covered with a layer of earth so that everyone could forget it was there, became the number one method of waste disposal. They have remained so ever since.

By the late 1960s, however, a number of people had become concerned about the use of landfills. With the increasing cost of land making this method of trash disposal more expensive, people began to wonder: What is happening to all that crud down there in the landfills? How dangerous is the stuff that leaks out of them? And how can people justify tying up an ever-growing percentage of the planet's finite resources?

These questions were part of the growing environmental awareness that gave rise to Earth Day, a nationwide expression of concern about such issues as air and water pollution, energy conservation, wildlife preservation, and resource recovery. Organized by a coalition of environmental and citizens' groups,

A trash bin in East Germany. Unprepared for the deluge of consumer goods that came with the crumbling of East-West tensions, the designers of this trash bin will have to come up with a larger container.

the first Earth Day took place on April 22, 1970. The event is generally regarded as the birth of today's environmental movement. People began to talk about recycling glass, paper, and metal as an alternative method of trash disposal that would both conserve resources and reduce pollution.

Unfortunately, because many people in the early environmental movement were connected with the hippie subculture that flourished among American and European youth in the late 1960s and early 1970s, they were often dismissed by the business community, the government, and mainstream society as "flower children," "nature nuts," and "back-to-earthers." In truth, some environmentalists both then and now have proposed measures that are too extreme and impractical to be useful to society in general. But for the most part, the environmentalists of 20 years ago accurately predicted the garbage crisis that the world is facing today. They also told anyone who would listen that recycling could help solve the problem.

During the 1980s, more and more people began listening. With landfills closing on all sides and incinerators encountering widespread opposition, city and state officials, desperate to reduce the volume of trash, began passing recycling laws. Most of these laws require people to sort their trash into categories (such as paper, glass, and aluminum cans) before it is collected. This is called source separation, and it reduces sorting costs for the municipality and makes it easier to sell waste back to dealers or to industry. Industry, in turn, is under pressure to develop new technologies and products that will make efficient use of recycled trash. Where laws are not in place, individuals and neighbor-hoods have set up hundreds of voluntary recycling programs. Today, what most Americans and many people elsewhere in the world think of when they hear the word *recycling* is sorting their trash into categories and either placing it in special containers to be collected or taking it themselves to a collection center. This type of recycling—focusing on paper, glass, metal, and some plastics—diverts about 10% of U.S. waste from landfills and incinerators. Environmentalists, EPA officials, many elected leaders, and an increasing number of ordinary citizens say that the percentage should be much higher.

The 20th anniversary of Earth Day was celebrated on April 22, 1990. A flurry of books, newspaper and magazine articles, television specials, and news reports examined the state of the environment. Most reports that dealt with recycling presented the same verdict: Some progress has been made in the 20 years since the first Earth Day, but a very great deal remains to be done.

In this Milwaukee, Wisconsin, recycling plant, bundled papers are separated from the general flow of trash. When individual consumers separate papers from other waste items and bundle them up before collection, the cost of handling these materials is reduced.

P A P E R   A N D   O R G A N I C
W A S T E

Paper is the single biggest component of the world's garbage. It makes up 41% of all the trash produced in the United States. Paper trash includes books, magazines, office paper, junk mail, cardboard, and boxes. But the bulk of paper trash is newsprint. Fully 10% of all the garbage in the world consists of newsprint. Fortunately, newsprint and other types of paper are easily recyclable; unfortunately, much less waste paper is recycled than could be.

Throughout much of its history, the papermaking process resembled a kind of recycling in which trash, in the form of rags and plant waste such as straw, was turned into paper. Some of the earliest writing in the world was done on papyrus, a thin material made by weaving together strips cut from the stalk of a reed that grows in Egypt, and on parchment, or vellum, which is made from cured and scraped animal skins. Neither papyrus nor vellum is considered to be true paper, however, because paper is made by an entirely different process in which fibrous materials are shredded, moistened, mixed together, pounded flat, and then dried. The Chinese were the first to manufacture paper, probably in the 2nd century B.C. They used rags from worn-out silk and linen clothing, straw, and rice husks as the basis for their paper, sometimes adding fibers from bamboo cane. By the 8th century A.D., the art of papermaking had spread to the Arab peoples of western Asia, who used rags, flax (a plant used to make linen cloth), and cotton. For quite a long time, European papermakers also relied on rags, mostly of linen, with straw and grass added if rags were in short supply. Because few people could read and write, the raw material provided by worn-out linen clothing was generally enough to supply the papermaking industry. All paper was made by hand. But in the mid-15th century, Johannes Gutenberg invented printing with movable type, and the number of books in the world began to increase rapidly. So did the number of readers and writers, as education gradually became more universal.

The production of paper also rose sharply, especially after the first papermaking machine was developed in 1799. Rags, straw, and grass could no longer provide sufficient raw material. By the mid-19th century, papermakers had found a new raw material in wood. They developed the technology for extracting long, sturdy, organic fibers called cellulose from timber through a combination of pounding and chemical treatment. This wood pulp, as it is called, became the single biggest source of paper. By 1900, 60% of the raw material used in American paper was wood pulp, and the remaining 40% consisted of rags and recycled waste paper. Since then, the proportion of virgin—or non-recycled—materials in U.S. papermaking has remained high. Even during World War II, when the nation focused on recycling, only about 35% of the material used in papermaking was recycled.

If paper is not recycled, its only other source comes from the harvesting of the nation's virgin forests, perhaps even national parks and wilderness areas.

PAPER RECYCLING TODAY

Waste paper has long been used as a raw material for making new paper, although the recovery rate of waste paper—that is, the percentage of it that is recycled—has never been as high as modern environmentalists recommend. The principal kinds of waste paper used in papermaking are paper trimmings and shavings from printing plants; old books, magazines, and newspapers; paper bags, wrapping paper, cardboard boxes, and other paper packaging materials; writing or typing paper; and newsprint.

The treatment needed to make waste paper ready for a new use depends on the product that will be made from it. If waste paper is going to be made into coarse types of paper like roof shingles, cardboard packaging, or paperboard, little in the way of special treatment is required. The paper needs to be sorted, so that items such as plastic wrapping strips, paper clips, and staples can be removed. Then the paper is shredded, beaten into a fibrous pulp, and mixed with water and chemical preservatives in pulping machines. The pulp is pressed through giant rollers that flatten it into sheets and squeeze out moisture; it may also be dried in furnaces, with blasts of hot air. The paper is then cut to the desired size and shape and packaged for distribution.

Schoolchildren recycling paper during World War II. Awareness of a national emergency prompted widespread cooperation with recycling programs.

The conversion of waste paper to finer grades suitable for printing involves a few more steps. First, careful sorting is required. Waste paper is divided into categories such as newsprint; typing and computer paper; and magazines, which have shiny coated paper and colored inks and need special treatment. Next, the ink must be removed. This is done by soaking the paper and breaking it up into small pieces in giant washers, then treating it with chemicals that loosen the ink so that it can be rinsed away. Sometimes more than one such chemical must be used because many types of ink must be removed. Finally, the wet, shredded waste paper is blended with other materials according to the type of end product that is desired. Rags—which are still used to produce the finest, most expensive grades of paper—may be mixed in. Wood pulp and other forms of cellulose such as straw may also be added in varying proportions. If white paper or paper for greeting cards or stationery is to be produced, bleach may be added to lighten it; if newsprint is to be produced, a mixture of red and blue dyes is added to reduce the grayness of the final product. Chemical preservatives are also added.

At this point, the fully treated material is a sort of liquid sludge that is ready to be made into paper; papermakers call it "stuff." In most papermaking operations, the stuff passes through a machine called a beater, which is essentially a very heavy roller that presses the fibers in the stuff together and squeezes out the water. The paper is formed and held together by the natural interlocking of the long cellulose or rag fibers as they are pressed and dried. No glue is used in the process. In fact, the natural glue in wood, *lignin*, is removed chemically before the paper is made. A refining machine brushes the roll of stuff to smooth out

A mountain of cut logs awaits processing at a paper mill. Large machines convert the logs to wood chips, and chemical processes then make paper pulp. Recycling paper will reduce the amount of virgin logs needed for each batch of pulp.

A papermaking machine. Paper pulp, which has been chemically bleached white, sloshes out across a fast-moving, fine-mesh screen. The cellulose fibers align themselves with the mesh screen, forming the paper's grain. After warming, drying, pressing, and polishing, finished paper sheets are ready.

irregularities. The papermaking machine presses the stuff into thin slices, which are then further dried by pressing or in furnaces. Finally, the paper is polished or chemically treated to give it the proper finish and packaged as ordered by the customer, in cut sheets or rolls.

The papermaking process itself is pretty much the same whether one uses virgin materials, recycled materials, or a mixture of the two. The difference is in the preparation of the stuff. Recycled material requires careful sorting. This in turn means that the paper mill must have a place to store waste paper and the staff to sort it, as well as a means of disposing of waste paper that cannot be used. Removing ink from waste paper also requires special chemicals, equipment, and equipment operators. As a result, some paper mills are not set up to use any recycled materials, while others prefer to use virgin materials as much as possible. Another reason some papermakers like virgin materials is that they have a financial interest in cutting down trees. Some paper mills are owned by the same companies that own forests and logging services.

Not all paper products can be made with recycled paper. Brown grocery bags, for example, can be recycled *into* other types of paper, but they must be made, at least partially, *out of* virgin materials because only virgin materials have the long, unbroken fibers that give the bags their necessary strength. Unlike glass bottles and aluminum cans, which can be recycled an infinite number of times, paper cannot be recycled indefinitely. Each time it is recycled, its quality degrades slightly because the fibers become more and more broken. At some point recycled paper has to be mixed in with virgin material, and eventually after repeated uses, it ends up in a landfill or an incinerator.

Many paper mills in the United States and elsewhere use varying combinations of recycled and virgin materials. Environmentalists and the paper industry agree, however, that the best way to improve the recovery rate of waste paper is to build more mills designed to use only recycled material. In 1990, there were eight such mills in the United States, but several companies had announced plans to build large new ones. Since the late 1980s, however, paper recycling has been in trouble.

Because more people than ever are recycling paper, especially newsprint, its value in the marketplace has dropped. For years, many communities and organizations have been raising money by selling sorted and baled newspapers to dealers and paper mills for up to $20 a ton. But with the new wave of interest in recycling, fueled by both voluntary and mandatory recycling programs in cities and states nationwide, the volume of waste paper available for recycling skyrocketed. As a result, the dealers and mills found themselves with more waste paper on their hands than they could use. By early 1990, some communities that had formerly profited from the sale of waste paper were forced to pay $10 or more a ton to have used newspapers hauled away.

In order for recycling to remain an attractive alternative to landfills and incinerators, new markets must be found for waste paper. Otherwise, no matter how thoughtfully the waste paper is sorted and deposited in recycling centers by consumers, it will still be nothing but neatly packed trash. Currently, most concerned people agree that the biggest challenge is developing a strong market for used newsprint. This endeavor takes two forms. The first involves putting newsprint to new uses. Many farmers now use shredded newsprint, instead of straw, as bedding for livestock; afterward it is mixed with manure and blended into the soil. Scientists are also working to perfect methods of turning newsprint into ethanol, an alcohol compound that can be used for fuel. In addition, manufacturers are being urged to increase the amount of newsprint they use in such products as home insulation, wallboard, cardboard, tissue and toilet paper, and packaging materials.

The second way to increase the demand for used newsprint depends on the people who use it in the first place: the newspaper industry. American newspapers are the initial consumers of virtually all of the newsprint that is produced in the United States—more than 14 million tons in 1989. But only about 14% of all this newsprint is recycled into other newsprint. Several states have passed or are considering laws that would require newspaper publishers to increase the percentage of recycled newsprint used in their papers to between 35% and 50%. The American Newspaper Publishers Association opposes these laws, saying that government controls are unnecessary and impractical and that newspapers can improve the recovery rate voluntarily. The American Newspaper Institute, meanwhile, claims that the papermaking industry is doing enough. They estimate that the amount of used newsprint collected for recycling will total 8 million tons by 1994, up from 5.5 million tons in 1989, and that by 1994 the industry will have spent more than $1.1 billion on new plants and equipment specially designed to turn old newsprint into new newsprint.

Of course, newsprint is not the only kind of paper that can be recycled. Used cardboard boxes, sorted and baled, are sold to manufacturers who will recycle them into new boxes. These used boxes are big business. Selling for about $100 a ton in late 1989, used boxes are the port of New York's biggest export by volume. Most are sent to South Korea and Japan and return to the United States containing TVs and VCRs made in those countries. Another profitable area of paper recycling is typing and computer paper collected from offices. Some individuals and companies specialize in scavenging or brokering this high-quality waste paper, which sells for up to $200 a ton at the paper mills. But the key to continued success in the recycling of all types of paper is keeping the market value of recycled paper high, and the best way to do this, environmentalists say, is through consumer pressure for more recycled paper goods.

Bags of dead leaves about to be transported to compost heaps. Here organic materials decay naturally, producing high-quality fertilizer for lawns and gardens.

RECYCLING ORGANIC WASTE

Paper is an organic substance—that is, it is manufactured from material that was once alive. Recyclers, however, often apply the term *organic waste* specifically to food and lawn wastes. Lawn waste—grass clippings, trimmings from trees and shrubs, and fallen leaves—accounts for about 18% of the total American waste stream. In the fall, when huge quantities of leaves are raked and bagged for collection by disposal services, lawn waste makes up as much as 75% of the waste stream in some communities. Food waste—scraps from food preparation as well as uneaten food—accounts for another 8% of the waste stream. Organic waste thus makes up about 26% of the total waste stream—one-fourth of all trash. If this material were removed from the waste stream, the overall volume of trash would go down. In addition, the remaining trash would be easier to process because it would be drier and attract fewer flies, rats, and other vermin.

The best way to recycle organic garbage is by composting. Composting is the process that occurs in nature when vegetation decays on the ground. It produces a thick, moist type of soil called humus that is exceptionally rich in nutrients and can be used as fertilizer or soil conditioner for lawns and gardens. The composting process can be speeded up if organic waste is concentrated, or mixed with household wastes such as food scraps and pet manure, and supplied with the right amounts of sunlight, air, and water. This is usually done in a compost heap or compost pit.

People who have yards can do their own composting; it generally requires a space about five feet on each side, although some compost heaps are bigger. Numerous books about organic gardening and composting give detailed instructions for creating and maintaining a compost heap. But even apartment dwellers and people who do not want a compost pit of their own can recycle their organic waste with a little effort. Many communities have public composting centers. Individuals can put their lawn trimmings or food garbage into the communal pits and, if they wish, remove some humus for their own gardens. Local recycling centers, gardening shops, and city and state recycling agencies can usually provide information about composting programs.

Many countries around the world routinely recycle all kinds of organic waste. In countries where a large number of families still live on farms or in the country, scraps of food left by people are fed to the pigs, whose manure in turn serves as fertilizer. For thousands of years, the Chinese have practiced sewage gardening, in which human waste is systematically collected and used to fertilize fields and gardens. This type of recycling can spread disease, however, so only sewage that has been chemically treated to kill bacteria should be used on food crops. Most cities in China and India are surrounded by "green belts"—areas of market farms that absorb the organic waste of the cities for fertilizer. The Chinese are experimenting with new ways to conserve organic waste. For example, Shanghai, the most populous city in China, has a system in which organic garbage is hauled from apartment buildings to a communal compost heap outside town by tractors. The composting process releases methane gas, which is piped back into the apartments and used as fuel for cookstoves.

Organic waste seems at first glance to pose a less serious trash disposal problem than plastic milk jugs or aluminum beer cans because food and vegetation, by definition, are expected to

At this Department of Agriculture research center in Maryland, large compost heaps of sewage mixed with wood chips produce fertilizer and soil conditioner.

decompose easily and to be quickly reabsorbed into the natural cycle. But organic waste that is burned creates only ash (and is difficult to burn because it is damp), and organic waste that is landfilled may remain intact for decades. This is because the process of organic decomposition requires air and light, but the interiors of many landfills are airless and dark. Furthermore, most landfills are "sealed" from the surrounding environment by layers of clay or plastic film that are supposed to keep material from leaking out of them.

When landfills were introduced as a means of large-scale trash disposal, many people got the idea that paper and other organic trash in landfills would break down over time and be "returned to the land." In most cases, exactly the opposite occurs. Scientists who began excavating and studying the interiors of landfills in the 1980s were startled to find that apple cores deposited in the 1950s retained toothmarks nearly as sharp as the day they were eaten, and newspapers from the 1960s could still be read. Today there is growing awareness that throwing trash—even easily biodegradable trash like food—into a landfill is a good way to keep it around for a long, long time.

FAST FACTS ABOUT PAPER RECYCLING

- People in the United States use about 50 million tons of paper—and 850 million trees—each year. This equals about 580 pounds of paper for each American each year. Roughly 120 pounds of this is newsprint.
- The average household throws away 13,000 separate pieces of paper each year. Most is packaging and junk mail.

- The Sunday papers published in the United States each week use the pulp from 500,000 trees; the *New York Times* Sunday edition alone requires 75,000 trees—in part because the *Times* uses only 8% recycled newsprint.
- Recycling 1 ton of paper spares 17 trees, which can absorb a total of 250 pounds of carbon dioxide from the air each year. Burning that same ton of paper creates 1,500 pounds of carbon dioxide, which contributes to pollution by greenhouse gases.
- Recycling paper uses about half as much energy as manufacturing paper from virgin materials.
- In 1989, the EPA estimated that Americans recycled 26% of their waste paper.

An endless stream of soft-drink cans moves along a conveyer belt in this
aluminum recycling plant.

chapter 4

GLASS AND METAL

Two kinds of waste that have been successfully recycled for some time are glass containers and metal (especially aluminum beverage cans). Unlike paper, both glass and metal can be recycled an infinite number of times and do not degrade, so that products made from recycled glass or metal are indistinguishable from products made from virgin materials.

Glass makes up 8% of the total U.S. waste stream. This waste consists of many different types of glass products: bottles, jars, light bulbs, broken windows, glassware used in cooking, and drinking glasses. Not all of this glass is recyclable, however, because different products require slightly different manufacturing processes.

Glass manufacturing has been carried on for thousands of years. Although glassmaking today is a sophisticated technology that takes place in large, expensive plants, the basic process is the same as it was in ancient times. Certain minerals and compounds—mostly white sand, soda, and lime, with various oxides to produce colors—are combined and heated at temperatures as high as 2,500 degrees Fahrenheit. The heat melts the ingredients, fusing them together to form a clear, transparent liquid. When this liquid is cooled, it forms a brittle, transparent substance.

For centuries, glassmakers have practiced recycling. Broken glass left over from the manufacturing process is added to the raw materials that are being heated. This broken glass is called "cullet." When cullet is used, the materials melt and fuse more quickly and at lower temperatures. Using cullet—that is, recycling broken glass—thus saves energy and time for glassmakers. Container glass can be made entirely from cullet, which requires only about two-thirds as much energy as glass made from virgin materials. For this reason, glassmaking companies and scrap dealers are generally interested in buying glass that can be made into cullet.

At this time, only glass bottles and jars are used as cullet. Window glass, glass cookware, and lightbulbs are specially treated and cannot be mixed in with other kinds of glass. Crystal drinking glasses also fall into this category. Recycling efforts, therefore, generally concentrate on glass food and beverage containers. Most of these are either clear, green, amber, or brown. Glassmakers, recycling firms, and cullet dealers use large magnets to remove metal caps from broken glass (although it helps if the consumer has already removed all metal parts). Special vacuums and filters are used to remove paper labels and plastic foam coatings. Some recycling programs require consumers to sort glass by color.

Bottle laws have greatly increased glass recycling. These laws require consumers to pay a deposit on beverages in glass bottles, which is refunded when the bottles are returned to the store. The idea is that if the actual consumers are not sufficiently interested in returning their bottles, other people may scavenge

This truck is collecting glass bottles for recycling. Because the color of the glass indicates different chemical compositions, it is important to sort glass by color before recycling.

The materials needed to make glass: sand (silica), limestone, and recycled glass bits, or cullet. These materials are melted together in a furnace at a temperature of 2,500 degrees Fahrenheit.

the bottles from litter or trash in order to get the deposits, so the glass will be removed from the waste stream one way or another. The first bottle law in the United States was introduced in Oregon in 1972. Since then, eight other states have passed bottle laws: Connecticut, Michigan, Delaware, Iowa, Maine, Massachusetts, Vermont, and New York. Bottle laws originally covered only glass bottles but now apply to aluminum beverage cans and plastic soda bottles as well.

The supporters of bottle laws claim that they are highly successful. Jon Naar, author of *Design for a Livable Planet,* says that New York's bottle law, which was enacted in 1983, saved $50 to $100 million in energy costs, $50 million in cleanup costs, and $19 million in solid waste disposal costs during its first 2 years. According to the EarthWorks Group in Berkeley, California, states with bottle laws have reduced their solid waste by 8% and their litter by about 50%. And the Environmental Action Foundation reports that states with bottle laws achieve a recovery rate of 90% for glass bottles and beverage cans and 70% for plastic soda bottles. But the Glass Packaging Institute states that bottle laws, or forced deposit laws, can have a negative effect on recycling because they take glass and metal containers— traditionally among the most profitable sectors of the recycling industry—away from municipal or community voluntary recycling programs, so that some of these programs fail. Many states are still debating whether to introduce bottle laws.

FAST FACTS ABOUT GLASS RECYCLING

° Making glass causes air and water pollution. Using recycled glass instead of virgin material in the

glassmaking process cuts related air pollution by 20%
and related water pollution by 50%.

° Mining and transporting raw materials produces about
385 pounds of waste for every ton of glass that is made.
If recycled glass is substituted for half of the virgin
materials, the waste is cut by more than 80%.

° Glass breaks down into its component elements very,
very slowly. It would probably take a modern glass
bottle 4,000 years or more to decompose—even longer
if it is in a landfill.

° Recycling glass saves energy. Processing containers as
trash takes three times as much energy as reusing them.
Enough energy is saved by recycling a single glass
bottle to light a 100-watt light bulb for 4 hours.

° According to the National Consumers League, about
one-third of all the glass on supermarket shelves is
made from recycled glass.

° Each year, Americans throw away 28 billion glass
bottles and jars. The EarthWorks Group calculates that
this is enough glass to fill both towers of the World
Trade Center in New York City 26 times.

° The recovery rate for glass in the United States was 9%
in 1989.

MINING METAL TRASH

About 9% of the total U.S. waste stream consists of metal.
Much of it is recyclable. The easiest kinds of metal to recycle are
aluminum and steel. Some tin is recycled along with steel,
because some food cans are made of both metals, and a few other
metals, such as copper, are salvaged by scrap dealers.

Industry, government, and environmentalists agree: Aluminum cans are recycling's biggest success story. These beverage cans account for most metal recycling. They can be endlessly recycled, and the process is quick. Cans collected for recycling are passed through a magnetic screening process that lifts out any nonaluminum materials. The cans are then flattened, shredded into small chips about the size of cornflakes, and melted down. At this point recycled aluminum is exactly like virgin aluminum made from bauxite, an earthy ore that contains aluminum oxides and is increasingly expensive to mine and transport. The recycled aluminum is rolled out into large sheets and then shaped into the desired product. The entire recycling process—from the moment when a customer buys a can of soda to the moment when a new can made from the same material appears on the grocer's shelf—can take as little as 90 days. Making a can from recycled aluminum takes only one-twentieth of the total energy required to make a can from bauxite. It also creates about one-twentieth as much air pollution. Other aluminum products such as pie plates, convenience food trays, siding, window frames, old ladders, automobile bumpers, and lawn furniture frames can also be recycled, providing they are 100 percent aluminum.

Aluminum recycling succeeds for a very simple reason: It makes money. Mining bauxite is expensive—much more expensive than recycling aluminum. Aluminum manufacturing companies like Reynolds Aluminum and Alcoa have found that it is cheaper for them to encourage and support recycling programs and to pay for recycled cans than to mine new bauxite. The aluminum industry operates more than 10,000 collection points, or buy-back centers, across the country where cash is paid on the spot for cans. Some of these buy-back centers have reverse vending machines, in which consumers deposit their cans. The cans are magnetically screened and weighed, and the machine issues a cash payment.

In early 1990, cans were bringing in 30 to 40 cents a pound, and 94,000 of them were being recycled every minute. In addition to people who save their own cans and turn them in for money, many people scavenge cans from trash containers, beaches, sports stadiums, parks, and other places. Not only does

In many areas, collecting deposits from glass bottles and metal cans is providing a small, extra source of income for the poor and the homeless.

A large-scale iron and steel scrap processing operation. The piles of scrap metal in the background will be pressed into the bales visible in the foreground and then shipped to various industries.

this reduce litter and solid waste, but many homeless people manage to earn some cash by can picking. On a larger scale, churches, social groups, and charities often raise funds through can drives. Cities and townships sell the cans that are collected through their recycling programs to industry to help pay the costs of operating the programs, or, in some cases, to earn a profit. The pickings from can picking are not small. In 1989, the aluminum industry paid out more than $900 million for 49.4 billion used cans, almost 2 billion pounds of them. Since can recycling started in the early 1970s, more than 360 billion cans—enough to reach to the moon and back 113 times—have been recycled, for a total payout of $4 billion.

Steel is also recycled, generally by scrap dealers who purchase it from recycling programs. Scrap steel has always been an ingredient in the manufacture of new steel, and today steel food cans, automobile parts, girders from torn-down buildings, and other kinds of steel trash are made into new products. Most steel manufactured today includes at least 25% used steel. According to the Steel Can Recycling Institute, the amount of steel that is recycled each year is equal to about one-third of all the solid waste that is landfilled, so recycling steel dramatically reduces the waste stream. The institute estimates that steel recycling during the 1980s extended the useful lifetime of United States landfills by more than three years.

FAST FACTS ABOUT METAL RECYCLING

- The recovery rate for aluminum cans in the United States in 1989 was 60.8%—the highest of any recyclable product. This was up from 54.6% in 1988 and 50.5% in 1987.

- Aluminum can recycling in 1989 saved enough energy to supply a city the size of Pittsburgh with power for three years.
- Throwing a single aluminum can away instead of recycling it wastes as much energy as it takes to run a television set for about three hours. Recycling one can saves the equivalent of half a gallon of gasoline.
- Aluminum degrades very slowly under natural conditions. A can that is thrown away will still be a can 500 years from now.
- Cans for recycling should be rinsed and dried. Most collection locations deduct 10% from the buy-back payment for dirty or wet cans. Cans are easier to store and transport if they are crushed flat.
- Recycling cans instead of manufacturing them from raw materials reduces related air pollution and energy expenditure by 95%.
- Can use is growing. Nearly 83 million aluminum beverage cans were sold in the United States in 1989—a 9.6% increase over 1988.
- Because so many of them are recycled, aluminum cans account for less than 1% of the total U.S. waste stream, according to EPA estimates.
- Recycling a ton of aluminum saves 4 tons of bauxite and more than 1,000 pounds of petroleum products.
- Recycling a ton of steel produces 200 fewer pounds of air pollutants, 100 fewer pounds of water pollutants,

and 3 fewer tons of mining waste than manufacturing
the same ton of steel from raw materials.
° The energy saved each year by recycling steel is
sufficent to supply power to Los Angeles for eight years.
Recycling 1 pound of steel saves enough energy to light
a 60-watt light bulb for 26 hours.

Crushed plastic containers are separated from the waste stream. Plastic is one of the most problematic materials to recycle.

P L A S T I C S

Plastic has always been the biggest problem faced by the recycling movement. Although plastic makes up only 7% of the total solid waste stream by volume, it is highly visible in trash and garbage for several reasons. For one thing, plastic has replaced many other items, such as glass bottles and paper bags, that can more easily be recycled. For another, plastic is often used in fast-food containers, disposable consumer goods, and convenience products in general—prominent symbols of the throwaway thinking that has contributed so greatly to the garbage crisis. Furthermore, plastic is very slow to break down, especially in landfills, and some types of plastic never degrade. Finally, most people are aware that paper, glass, and metal *can* be recycled, even if they do not themselves take part in recycling. But recycling plastic is technologically difficult and expensive—and, unlike glass and metal, plastic can be recycled only once.

There are between 45 and 50 types of plastic in commercial use today. Although some plastics are made partly of organic materials such as cellulose, most of them are made of polymers, molecular compounds produced by industrial processes involving heat and chemical treatment. Essentially,

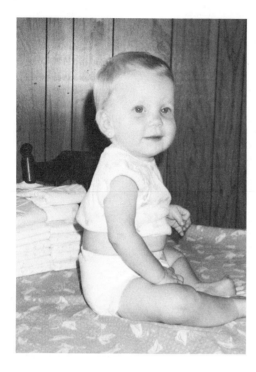

Plastic disposable diapers may be a great convenience for parents, but they are not so easily disposable after they have been collected from individual households.

most plastics consist of acids and petroleum by-products. These are heat treated and chemically processed to form liquid substances called resins. The resins are then shaped into products by a variety of machines: rollers, extruders (which squeeze liquid plastic out through narrow openings under pressure), and molds. Because the process of making plastic permanently alters the chemical characteristics of the resins, the ways in which plastics can be recycled are limited, and some plastics cannot be recycled with existing technology. Moreover, even those plastic items that are recyclable generally cannot be reused for their initial purposes. When recycled, they form a somewhat different type of plastic, with different uses. As a result, recycling plastic is an expensive effort. New product uses must be developed.

One of the problems with plastics recycling is that different kinds of plastic are made from different resins. To be recycled effectively, they need to be identified and sorted properly, but consumers do not know how to do this. The plastics industry has developed a code to identify seven general categories of plastic that are used in food and beverage packaging and other consumer goods. These symbols are beginning to appear on recyclable plastics. The seven categories are as follows:

1. *Polyethylene terephthalate*, or PET (which has the code PETE). This is the material from which large plastic soda bottles are made. It is the most recycled kind of plastic in the world today. Slightly more than 20% of all PET bottles are recycled, and more than 90% of those that are recycled are collected in states with bottle laws.

2. *High-density polyethylene* (code HDPE). This is a version of PET that is used to make thick, rigid containers such as milk and water jugs and bottles for detergent and other household supplies.

3. *Polyvinyl chloride*, or PVC (code V). This plastic, often called simply vinyl, is used in rigid form to make bottles, pipes, tubes, molded furniture, and automobile parts. In the form of thin film, it is used for grocery bags and other packaging materials. Much of it is used in construction and industry. Although it can be recycled, very little of it is currently reused.

4. *Low-density polyethylene* (code LDPE). This plastic is used in trash bags, photographic films, and disposable diapers and has many industrial uses.

5. *Polypropylene* (code PP). This plastic has many industrial and commercial uses. It is used for special types of

clothing and in bottles that can be recycled, but the demand for it by recyclers is low.

6. *Polystyrene* (code PS). This plastic is most familiar to consumers as polystyrene foam, often called by its trade name of Styrofoam. Polystyrene foam is used for fast-food packages, trays in which meat is packaged in supermarkets, and packing materials (usually called "peanuts" or "chips"). It can be recycled, but the amount currently recycled is small.

7. All other resins and layered or combined materials (code Other). These products do not lend themselves to recycling because they generally consist of multiple resins that are not easily separated.

Once plastics—PET soda bottles, for example—have been sorted, either by consumers at a recycling center or by dealers, they are "densified" to eliminate the volume taken up by the air they hold. This just means that they are flattened and mashed together. Then they are tied into bales and shipped to processing plants.

At the plants, plastics are chopped into small pieces (called "chips"), washed, and dried. At this point, plastic can be processed in many ways. Some plastic is shredded into fine particles to be used as carpet backing, felt casings on tennis balls, or filler for parkas and sleeping bags. Some of it is molded by heat and pressure into lengths like boards for use in construction or as fence posts, park benches, automobile curbs in parking lots, and boat docks. And some of it—often mixed with new resins—is made into consumer goods such as rigid bottles and pails. But federal regulations for food packaging prohibit recycled plastic being used in food or beverage containers.

CHALLENGES IN PLASTICS RECYCLING

The recycling of plastic has lagged behind that of paper, glass, and metal because plastic cannot be reused as readily. But the production and use of plastic rises steadily each year. The EPA estimates that the amount of plastic trash generated in 1990 will be doubled by 2000. Environmentalists and the plastics industry agree that more plastic must be removed from the waste stream. They differ, however, on how this goal should be accomplished.

Most environmentalists recommend that society should modify its dependence on plastic. They would like to see lots of plastic, particularly in packaging, replaced by materials such as paper, glass, and metal that are easier to recycle, do not use up as many petroleum products, and produce fewer by-products from chemical reactions. Environmentalists also support a move toward refillable plastic bottles for some products, such as water, household cleaners, motor oil, and the like; this would encourage consumers to use their bottles over and over again.

The plastics industry, on the other hand, points out that because of its low weight, plastic accounts for a relatively small percentage of the total waste stream. Industry experts also claim that new technology and improved collection systems will allow plastics to be more efficiently and economically recycled. A coalition of plastics industry organizations predicts that plastics recycling will increase by 31% each year from 1990 to 1994.

The industry's desire to improve its recycling performance is in part the result of consumer pressure and environmental concerns, but also because of some new or proposed laws. A few communities have passed or are considering ordinances that ban certain types of plastic packaging. Suffolk County, New York, for

In Elburn, Illinois, these environmentally concious teenagers have collected a mountain of polystyrene to be recycled at the Landfill Alternatives recycling plant.

example, banned polystyrene foam, but the ban has been postponed because of stiff opposition from manufacturers, stores, and restaurants. Many more areas are including PET bottles and some other types of plastic in their recycling programs. This will create a supply of used plastic, and the plastics industry will risk sharp criticism from environmental groups if it does not take steps to absorb recycled plastic. But because it is not indefinitely recyclable, plastic continues to pose a long-term disposal problem. The industry is concentrating on finding ways to use recycled plastics in products that have long lifetimes, such as fencing and road-building material.

For the 1990s, the two most controversial subjects in the field of plastics disposal and recycling are likely to be degradable plastics and polystyrene foam. Degradable plastics have been developed by the plastics industry in response to public demand for plastics that are less damaging to the environment. There are two types: photodegradable and biodegradable.

Photodegradable plastics are supposed to break up when exposed to sunlight, which weakens the chemical links that bind plastic components together. These plastics were hailed as a way to reduce litter on beaches and in public places—the trash would simply dissolve under the open sky. Some states have already passed laws that require six-pack rings to be made of photodegradable plastic. But as environmentalists point out, these plastics do not really disappear. They break up into smaller pieces, and a residue of polystyrene and other chemicals remains. The photodegradable plastics may be solving a litter problem merely by moving the waste disposal dilemma further down the line.

Biodegradable plastics contain a high percentage of cornstarch and are supposed to decay naturally, like organic material. They are being used in disposable diapers and in the type of trash bags used for putting lawn waste in compost heaps. But these plastics degrade best under laboratory conditions; no one knows how well they will perform in landfills, where even food and newspapers can linger stubbornly intact for decades. And as with photodegradables, some resin and chemical residues remain when biodegradable plastics break down. The long-term hazards of these residues are unknown. In addition, the environmental problem caused by disposable diapers includes not just the diapers themselves but also the infectious human waste they introduce into landfills. Currently about 3% of all landfill leachate consists of such waste.

The plastics industry introduced degradable plastics with a great fanfare, but even the companies that invented them now admit that they are a partial and incomplete solution whose long-term usefulness is doubtful. Furthermore, degradables increase the difficulty of recycling regular plastic. If a load of recycled plastic being reprocessed into resins happens to include some degradable plastic items, the entire batch of resin will be ruined. Another drawback to degradable plastics is that the liberal use of terms such as *biodegradable diaper* and *photodegradable plastic* gives many people the false impression that science has solved the problem and that plastic will now break down harmlessly into the environment. This misconception may cause people to slack off on proper trash disposal and recycling efforts. The overall effect of degradable plastics may be to set back plastics recycling in general.

Polystyrene foam is another problem area, and one in which the battle line is sharply drawn between the plastics industry and environmentalists, who maintain that polystyrene foam creates serious problems connected with pollution, litter, and waste disposal. Their arguments are as follows: Polystyrene is made from benzene, a proven cause of cancer, and from various gases, which give it its foamy texture. The gases most often used are chlorofluorocarbons (CFCs), harmful substances that nibble away at the ozone layer in the atmosphere and contribute to the greenhouse effect and global warming. Sometimes other gases are used in place of CFCs, but they are sources of urban smog. Hazardous dioxin is produced as a by-product of making polystyrene. Polystyrene foam takes up excessive space in landfills even when it is crushed because the material itself contains so much air. Carelessly discarded polystyrene foam sometimes breaks up into small pellets; birds and fish mistake these pellets for food and die from eating them.

Polystyrene foam is well entrenched in the fast-food industry. It offers great advantages: It is cheap, convenient, lightweight, and unbreakable. The McDonald's hamburger chain alone used about 70 million pounds of polystyrene in 1989. Aware of the attacks on polystyrene foam by environmentalists, the fast-food and plastics industries have launched several joint ventures intended to prove that polystyrene can be successfully recycled. One such program under way in Brooklyn, New York, takes in trash bags from 19 McDonald's locations, sorts the polystyrene foam, and prepares it to be reprocessed into construction material and rigid plastic items such as trays and pails. A company called Plastics Again in Leominster, Massachusetts, has pioneered the commercial recovery of polystyrene foam. The company is owned by a coalition of 8 manufacturers of polystyrene foam who have announced a joint

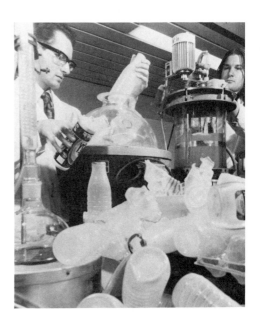

The medical school at the University of Manchester in England has conducted experiments using microbes to break down plastic. One of the end products is a protein that may be used as food for cattle.

A vast field of used automobile tires in Green Swamp, Florida. Rubber is difficult to break down without producing toxic substances, but it is a useful construction material.

goal of recycling 25% of their product by 1995. Researchers at GE Plastics, a division of General Electric, are studying the possibility of making houses and cars from recycled plastic. But it remains to be seen how effective such pilot programs will be in reducing waste—and in any case none of these programs address the growing problem of chemical pollution created by the production of polystyrene and other plastics.

Rubber is not a true plastic, but it poses similar waste disposal and recycling challenges. The biggest source of waste rubber is discarded tires—some 220 million of them each year in the United States alone. They are vexing to landfill operators because, like the vampires of legend, they refuse to stay decently buried. Their hollow inner surfaces trap gases and pull them persistently to the tops of even the deepest landfills, and they do not decompose. But rubber can be recycled, and recycling a pound of rubber saves 71% of the energy needed to produce a pound of virgin rubber. Fortunately, tire recycling is on the increase. Most tires manufactured today contain no more than

10% recycled rubber, but environmental experts claim that this could be raised as high as 30% with no loss of tire safety or performance.

Ground-up used rubber, called "crumb" rubber, can be added to asphalt paving on roads, playgrounds, and parking lots. Additional uses for this rubber are found in adhesives, insulation, hoses, carpet padding, and sports equipment. Crumb rubber has also been used to manufacture rubber substitutes, such as those marketed under the Tirecycle brand.

FAST FACTS ABOUT PLASTICS RECYCLING

- The recovery rate for plastics in the United States in 1989 was 1%, according to the Environmental Action Foundation.
- In 1989, the Du Pont company, the largest plastics maker in the United States, announced plans to build several large plastics recycling centers that will recycle a total of 40 million tons of plastic each year by 1995.
- More than 25 billion polystyrene foam containers are manufactured each year in the United States alone.
- In 1989, the total number of discarded rubber tires being held in storage facilities in the United States was well over 2 billion.
- A major use for recycled PET plastics is in the manufacture of polyester fibers. About 35% of the polyester carpeting made in the United States contains some recycled material.

The message is clear, but the ground around the trash bin shows that not everyone has hit the bull's-eye.

D O E S   R E C Y C L I N G
M A K E   A   D I F F E R E N C E ?

Recycling can make a difference, as people around the globe are discovering. Recycling programs both large and small have skimmed up to 40% off the waste streams of communities, cities, and nations. Even the most pessimistic projection for overall, global solid waste reduction—that of the National Solid Waste Management Association in the United States—says that recycling can cut waste by 20%. The Center for the Biology of Natural Systems at Queens College in New York speculates that as much as 88% of solid waste could be recycled if people were fully motivated, and if society and the marketplace put a sufficiently high value on recycled goods.

In 1988, the EPA set a goal of reducing the nation's solid waste by 50% by 1992. EPA experts hoped that half of that target reduction would be achieved by more and better recycling. Some states, cities, and townships have set even more ambitious goals for themselves, planning to recycle 40% or even 50% of their waste by the mid-1990s. In 1991, it is too soon to tell how many of these goals will be reached, but the final years of the 1980s saw a boom in recycling programs. In the April 1990 issue of

BioCycle magazine, Jim Glenn reported that more than 1,500 curbside recycling projects and nearly 1,000 yard-waste composting projects were operating in the United States. Both numbers were up by about 50% from 1988, and both are expected to grow throughout the 1990s.

Recycling programs fall into two broad classifications: voluntary and mandatory. Most voluntary recycling occurs when individuals or families collect and sort their trash and take recyclables to drop-off points. Some drop-offs handle just one resource, such as the buy-back locations for aluminum cans. Other drop-offs, including many run by churches, community organizations, and municipalities, accept more than one kind of material. Sometimes the consumer has to separate the recyclables, and sometimes the drop-off center has a sorting staff. Recyclables collected at these drop-off points are sold to dealers or directly to industry. Some large drop-off centers are called MRFs, or mass regional facilities. These are generally operated for profit by states or private companies, and they accept all sorts of recyclables, sometimes paying consumers for them. A few voluntary programs offer what is called curbside recycling, in which sorted recyclables are picked up from consumers' homes.

Curbside recycling, however, is more often associated with mandatory recycling programs—that is, with programs that are required by law. Mandatory recycling involves a complex and often confusing web of legislation at the state, county, and municipal levels. There are three basic types of recycling laws. One type deals only with recycling and usually sets a goal in terms of the percentage of solid waste that is to be recycled or the desired recovery rates of recyclables. A second type sets target goals for landfilling and incineration along with recycling. The

A typical curbside recycling program in action. Different categories of trash will be collected on different days.

third and most ambitious type of law includes goals for composting and also for the overall reduction of the waste stream through changes in packaging, manufacturing, and consuming habits.

The states of New Jersey, New York, Pennsylvania, and Rhode Island and the District of Columbia have laws that require all municipalities with populations of 5,000 or more to pass local recycling laws by certain deadline dates; many of these local ordinances have already been enacted. The states of Connecticut, Maryland, Minnesota, North Carolina, Oregon, and Washington have laws that require local governments to develop recycling programs by deadline dates—although there is no requirement

Neighborhood recycling centers such as this one in Greenwich Village in New York City attempt to make the collection and separation of trash more convenient for urban residents.

that the programs actually be put into action. California, Florida, Louisiana, Ohio, Vermont, and Virginia have laws that require local governments to reach waste reduction goals—using whatever means they choose—by deadline dates. Illinois, Iowa, and Michigan have laws that require local governments to include recycling in all plans for solid waste disposal. Even in states that do not have statewide recycling laws, counties and municipalities can enact their own mandatory programs, and many have done so. All states and most cities and counties have recycling agencies, some of which operate active programs and some of which provide information only. Information about recycling is also available from many environmental groups and from the EPA and its regional offices.

In areas where recycling is mandatory, it is generally carried out through curbside collection. Sometimes all trash is collected at once, with recyclables sorted and separated from other trash, often in distinctive containers provided by the collection service. In other cases, different types of trash are collected on different days: glass on Wednesday, for example, cans on Thursday, and unsorted trash on Friday. Of course, there are no "trash police" to come into people's homes and force them to comply with recycling laws.

Some communities interpret "mandatory recycling" to mean simply that recycling programs must be available for people who *want* to use them. But many communities do enforce the laws, either by charging householders extra to have unsorted trash collected or by not picking up any trash from households that do not recycle. Another method of enforcing compliance was adopted by the town of High Bridge, New Jersey, which used to charge each household $200 a year for trash removal. Now it sells each household 52 plastic stickers for $200. The town will pick up any bag or can of unsorted trash with a sticker on it. Households that can make their supply of 52 stickers last longer than a year therefore save money, and one of the easiest ways to do this is to separate recyclables.

Just as there are many different types of recycling laws and collecting systems, the materials covered by mandatory recycling programs are different from place to place. Nearly all programs cover aluminum cans, glass containers, and newspapers. Some cover all kinds of paper and metal trash. More and more of them are adding lawn waste (for composting) and certain plastics, especially PET.

Recycling efforts are often combined with other social concerns. Some drop-off centers are operated by environmental organizations that put the profits into such projects as wildlife preservation or clean-air campaigns. Other recycling centers are found in shelters for the homeless or for women and children; the people who live in the shelter do the sorting and the profits help pay the shelter's expenses. A number of cities and towns have programs in which recyclable materials are set aside to help the homeless or provide for charities. Some communities have established informal networks to collect cans and put them where homeless people can gather them. Social consciousness plays a part in recycling on the corporate level, too, as in the case of utilities companies that burn trash for fuel and hire the unemployed or homeless to sort the trash and separate recyclables.

An innovative Canadian recycling program based on cooperation between government and private industry is described in *Coming Full Circle*, a book on waste management published in 1988 by the Environmental Defense Fund. In the province of Ontario, the Ministry of the Environment and a group of corporations set up a plan that initially involved 1.2 million households. Twenty corporations that manufacture aluminum cans and beverages contributed $20 million to help pay for weekly curbside collection of beverage cans from special containers; the province kicked in $40 million. The program has been successful, and the Ministry of the Environment expects that all of Ontario's 9 million households will be participating in the

Franklin, Ohio, has named itself Environmental City because it was the first city to initiate total recycling of all its wastes at its new automated plant.

recycling program by the mid-1990s. Canada's other provinces are testing several types of recycling programs, both mandatory and voluntary.

TWO SUCCESS STORIES

Recycling programs can work in small towns or sprawling metropolises, as the cases of North Stonington, Connecticut, and Seattle, Washington, demonstrate.

In 1983, North Stonington had a population of 4,300, a 40-year-old landfill, and a town government that consisted of 3 part-time officials. One selectman, David Birkbeck, was given responsibility for the dump, which was expected to be full by 1990. Although he did not know much about recycling, he was determined to extend the lifetime of the landfill by reducing the amount of trash put into it. Otherwise, the town would be forced to spend a lot of money to have its trash hauled elsewhere for disposal. So Birkbeck started a one-man, hands-on operation by climbing into the dump and weeding out cardboard, newspapers, and bottles to be recycled. He buttonholed his fellow citizens on the street and talked them into voluntarily sorting their trash. He wrote passionate editorials about recycling for the local paper. He studied the recycling industry and worked hard to find customers for the recyclables he gathered. Eventually his operation began to make a little money for the town, which was then able to pay workers to sort and to make deliveries to dealers.

Sorting and recycling became a way of life for the people of North Stonington, who appreciated its straightforward financial benefits. North Stonington became one of the first Connecticut communities to consider passing a recycling law. A town meeting was held to vote on the law, and the only negative vote came from the local trash collector. Three years after the law was passed, an environmental consultant estimated that recycling had cut the amount of waste entering North Stonington's landfill by 65%, extending the landfill's life by perhaps as much as 40 years and saving the town $50,000 a year.

The city of Seattle turned to recycling in desperation in the 1980s, when plans were under way to build a huge new incinerator to handle the city's burgeoning waste load. Fears of toxic pollution and other problems connected with incineration made residents wary, and the mayor agreed to delay the planned construction until 1996 if a comprehensive recycling program was started instead. Environmentalists and city governments agree that the success of Seattle's recycling effort is inspiring.

Seattle has experimented with several different methods of collecting recyclables. In the northern part of the city, households sort their own trash, placing cans, bottles, paper, and newsprint in color-coded containers provided by the city. In the southern part, residents put all recyclables into a single large can, and the contents are sorted later at a central processing facility. Residents receive monthly bills from the city for the disposal of unsorted trash. They are charged according to the size and number of cans they use: the less trash, the lower the charge. This motivates people to separate their recyclables to keep trash collection costs down. Once these programs were up and running, Seattle began collecting and composting yard waste.

By early 1990, five years after starting its recycling drive, Seattle had achieved an exceptionally high rate of participation. More than 60% of the city's households were recycling, and more than 30% of all household garbage was being recycled—2,500 tons of bottles, cans, and paper every month. Seattle is aiming still higher, however. According to the January/February 1989 issue of *Greenpeace* magazine, the city's goal is to recover 60% of its total waste stream.

AN INTERNATIONAL PERSPECTIVE

Some other nations are more successful than the United States in achieving high recycling rates. Per person, the citizens of Japan, West Germany, the Netherlands, and Italy recycle twice as much as Americans do—mostly to save energy. German and French engineers have developed sophisticated trash-sorting equipment that uses lasers to identify recyclables quickly and easily. Denmark has an efficient garbage collection system that uses trash bags made out of moisture-resistant paper. The bags allow moisture to evaporate, thus reducing the overall volume of the trash. The Danes are also champion recyclers of glass bottles and containers; according to Paul Connett of the Work on Waste organization, the recovery rate for these items in Denmark is 99.6%.

Most industrialized nations equal or surpass the United States in recycling, but the developing nations of Africa, Asia, and Latin America have a growing waste problem. Because many of these countries are desperately trying to develop industries to support their populations, they often give environmental considerations second place or ignore them altogether. For example, chemical companies based in the United States and other industrialized countries can manufacture and sell many products in Third World nations that have been banned as too dangerous to be used at home.

Although the people of many Third World countries traditionally recycle usable or salable items as a matter of course, they have less experience in developing landfills, incinerators, sewage plants, and other modern waste disposal methods. Trash haulers from industrialized nations have exploited the Third World by dumping waste—often toxic and hazardous waste—in developing countries that are not equipped to handle it properly and do not have regulations against it. This practice is called "Third World dumping."

One of the most notorious cases of Third World dumping involved a ship called the *Khian Sea*, which picked up a load of 14,000 tons of toxic incinerator ash from Philadelphia in 1986. For two years the freighter roamed the seas, trying to find a country where it could dump its dangerous cargo. After being turned away from many ports, it dumped part of the ash on the beaches of Haiti in 1988, misrepresenting it as fertilizer. Then, after the ship's name was changed to *Pelicano*, probably in the hope of avoiding notoriety, the rest of the cargo was disposed of, although the captain refused to say where or how. The story of the *Khian Sea/Pelicano* roused worldwide indignation against the practice of Third World dumping. It also pointed out that waste disposal is no longer the concern of any single community or nation. It is a worldwide problem that demands international cooperation and global solutions.

No longer just an abstract problem, the trash crisis is now affecting life-styles and recreational habits. Medical waste, including possibly infectious materials, has closed this beach to swimmers.

TAMING THE WASTE STREAM

The average American produces 3.5 pounds of trash in a day, 24.5 pounds in a week, 1,277.5 pounds in a year, and 89,425 pounds over a 70-year life span. Although worldwide garbage production is difficult to calculate, experts agree that every person on the planet generates at least a pound of waste each day—significantly more than a pound in many cases. That means *at least* 5 billion pounds of new waste every day.

Recycling can divert a lot of this garbage from the waste stream. Government, industry, and environmentalists in many lands now agree that recycling must be an essential part of every waste control plan if the earth is to survive the trash crunch. But even if recycling programs were universal and operated at maximum efficiency—and this is a state of affairs that will probably never come to pass—there would still be waste that could not be recycled. Materials that currently cannot be safely or usefully recycled include hazardous and toxic chemicals, hospital and medical wastes, many plastics (especially those that contain several types of resins), ash, and thousands of disposable items that combine several elements, such as ballpoint pens made of plastic and metal. How can these items be disposed of?

Environmentalists like to describe the different methods of waste management as a ladder with three rungs. The bottom rung is for the least desirable methods of waste disposal, which are landfills and incinerators. These two methods are used for 90% of all U.S. solid wastes. Both are troublesome. Landfills are filling up fast, and it is increasingly difficult to find sites for new ones because public awareness of the problems they cause—as well as the negative effect they have on local property values—leads to NIMBY thinking at most proposed sites. And the landfills that

These construction workers are using a compound of recycled glass added to an asphalt base to fill potholes. Finding new uses for waste materials is an important part of the recycling effort.

already exist are leaking huge amounts of dangerous leachate into the nation's drinking water. The EPA has listed several thousand landfills as hazards to public health because they contain toxic chemicals or radioactive wastes that are inadequately protected. If landfills must be used, environmentalists say, they should be equipped with the best possible liners and seals and with pumps to drain out leachate—which, of course, poses another disposal problem.

Incinerators create problems, too, notably air pollution and piles of toxic ash that can be difficult to dispose of. And like landfills, incinerators often provoke a NIMBY reaction. But burning trash *does* produce energy, and supporters of incineration claim that an aboveground furnace is easier to operate safely than an underground landfill. Incinerators account for about 10% of waste disposal in the United States, but that percentage is much higher in Europe and Japan, partly because landfill space is even rarer there than in the United States. West Germany burns 34% of its trash for energy, Japan burns 33%, and Switzerland, which is generally regarded as a noticeably clean country, burns 75%.

Environmentalist Allen Hershkowitz of the National Resources Defense Council studied European incinerators and determined that incineration is safest and most efficient when the technology used in incinerators is up-to-date. It is important that only dry nonrecyclable trash be burned, that hazardous materials be removed before burning, that the incinerator's monitoring and scrubbing equipment be maintained by a highly trained staff, and that air pollution regulations be strict and strictly enforced. If incinerators are to be used more and more in the future, which seems likely, Hershkowitz recommends that a strong federal policy be developed to set standards and enforce them.

This plant in St. Louis, Missouri, processes trash for use as fuel by electric generating plants. It was the first such processing system in the United States.

The second rung on the waste management ladder is for methods that are more environmentally desirable than landfills and incinerators. These methods are recycling and composting, which recover resources for reuse, cut the volume of waste, save energy, and reduce pollution.

The top rung of the ladder is reserved for source reduction and precycling. Environmentalists now view source reduction as the single most promising and challenging aspect of the entire solid waste mess.

PRECYCLING BEFORE RECYCLING

The idea behind source reduction is simple: to prevent waste from being created rather than waiting to deal with it after it has been sitting around in big smelly piles for a week or a decade.

Basically, source reduction means designing, manufacturing, purchasing, and using products with the specific goal of reducing waste and pollution in mind at every step. In its most far-reaching form, source reduction means changing a social and economic philosophy based on consumption to one based on conservation. It calls for a reversal of the thinking that has built the "throwaway society." Naturally, no one expects a revolution in corporate ethics or in people's buying habits to take place overnight. But many aspects of source reduction can be put into practice at once by both manufacturers and consumers.

Manufacturers can evaluate every step of their operations with an eye toward reducing waste. This might mean changing some factory procedures or equipment so that less waste is generated. It might mean increasing the percentage of recycled raw materials used in the manufacturing process, so that fewer trees have to be logged or tons of ore mined. It might mean eliminating one layer of plastic or paper packaging, or replacing toxic inks and dyes on the package with less dangerous pigments. It might mean redesigning a product so that it is easier to repair and staffing repair facilities across the country. If these changes cost the manufacturers money, they will have to see how badly consumers want to reduce waste. Perhaps consumers would be willing to pay a little more for glass containers, for example, if they knew that glass recycling had reached a recovery rate of 90%.

From the consumer's point of view, source reduction might mean selecting products that use less packaging—fruits and vegetables chosen from bins, for example, instead of those in plastic bags or wrappers, or aspirin that comes in a tamper-proof bottle instead of aspirin that comes in a bottle inside a box inside

This billboard outside Denton, Texas, does not seem to be getting its message across.

plastic wrap. Environmentalists say that the easiest way to promote source reduction is to cut back on packaging, which makes up about 50% of all household trash by volume and 34% by weight. Every year, Americans discard an average of 600 pounds of packaging materials per person. A lot of this is food packaging. According to the Department of Agriculture, the United States spends more on packaging its food than all of the nation's farmers earn in combined net income. While some packaging is necessary, much of it exists only to attract attention to the product or for the convenience of manufacturers, shippers, and retailers.

The concept of source reduction has given rise to a new concept, that of precycling. Precycling is the task of each individual consumer. It means considering the waste potential of every purchase. A consumer who precycles asks him- or herself, Is this product reusable? Durable? Safe to use? Safe to discard? Is it recyclable? If not, could I substitute another product that is reusable or recyclable? Is this packaging necessary? If not, could I substitute a less heavily packaged product? These questions soon become automatic. Not every purchase will make good environmental sense, of course. Sometimes it is simply necessary or very much more convenient to buy something that will add to the waste stream. But people who precycle have less to recycle.

Activists from Greenpeace make their point at this beach on the island of Gibraltar in the Mediterranean.

chapter 8

TOWARD A REUSABLE WORLD

Recycling came of age in the United States in the 1980s.
First it was primarily the concern of environmentalists, scrap
dealers, and industries that traditionally used old materials, such
as glassmaking. By the end of the 1980s, however, it was being
discussed across the nation in town meetings, corporate
boardrooms, and government offices. Sorting their own trash and
separating recyclables is now a fact of life for millions of
Americans, as well as for restaurants, small businesses, schools,
and others whose trash is collected by municipal haulers.
Recalling the early days of the environmental movement, when
people who expressed concern for the environment were often
dismissed as "nature freaks," the authors of *Saving the Earth: A
Citizen's Guide to Environmental Action* describe recycling this
way: "It is no longer a chore for hippies only. Instead, what is
gradually emerging across the country is a broad recycling
structure initiated by government, private enterprise, and new
technology."

Three trends that gave direction to recycling in the 1980s
are likely to continue through the 1990s and beyond. One trend

involves legislation, one involves economics, and one involves technology. Together they will determine how widespread and effective recycling can become.

In terms of legislation, the late 1980s saw a sharp increase in the number of mandatory recycling programs. The early 1990s should see an even greater increase, as the towns and cities in states with statewide recycling or waste reduction laws rush to meet their state's deadlines for developing local programs. In addition, more states are expected to pass laws setting waste reduction or recycling goals that will have to be met by their towns and cities. And as trash disposal costs continue to rise and environmental consciousness grows, more towns and cities will act independently, passing recycling ordinances of their own in states that do not have statewide legislation.

Many communities are also attempting to pass laws to limit or ban particular elements of the waste stream. Several communities have tried to ban Styrofoam, for example, and several states have passed laws requiring newspaper printers to increase their use of recycled newsprint. For the most part, these laws have encountered delays and setbacks on their way to being enacted or enforced. Some of the laws have been suspended, and some of them have been challenged in court by manufacturer and retailer groups. These bans and limits are sometimes seen not so much as enforceable legislation but as communal statements of belief, much like the laws that have been passed declaring some towns "nuclear-free zones." Nevertheless, environmentalists are pushing for more such laws, hoping that they will spur changes in the ways manufacturers make and package their products.

On a larger scale, some environmentalists and waste disposal experts believe that it will not be possible to get the most

At this plant in Albany, New York, garbage is shredded and compacted and then burned to produce steam heat for state government office buildings.

out of recycling until the nation's legislators pass a strong federal recycling law. Such a law, environmentalists point out, would make recycling nationwide and would also make the country's recycling laws and methods more uniform. Traditionally, however, the federal government has left trash disposal largely up to the individual states, and this is unlikely to change in the near future. Environmentalists say, however, that even a nationwide recycling policy—a national plan or goal, if not a law—would help bring some order to the welter of different regulations, programs, and systems that govern recycling today. And beyond this national level are international concerns, such as Third World dumping, and pollution from incinerators and landfills that crosses national borders. A number of environmental organizations are international in scope, with members around the world, and some of them are calling for the heavily industrialized nations, the leaders in waste production, to lead the way toward a global waste policy.

The second major trend in recycling involves economics. Part of what has made recycling work is that it can be profitable—municipalities, scrap dealers, and individuals can earn money by recycling. The link between recycling and economics is shown by aluminum can recycling, which has succeeded because the aluminum industry has made it both easy and profitable for people to recycle their cans. Although the industrial giants of the glass, plastics, and paper industries do not yet support nationwide programs like that of the can industry, scores of new companies have sprung up from the country's trash heaps. These operations are the work of a new breed of recyclers who are sometimes called "enviro-entrepreneurs." They include a young man in Atlanta who started his own business buying used computer paper from companies (who would otherwise have to pay to have it disposed of by trash haulers) for 3 cents a pound and selling it to paper mills for 12 cents a pound; a New Jersey scrap metal dealer who boosted his sales to $2 million a year by adding glass to his operations; and a large recycling company, which was started by a manufacturer of aircraft products in Minnesota, that uses old motorized baggage carriers to haul recyclables around its plants. The growing interest in recycling as a business is shown in the recent increase in the number of subscribers to *Recycling Today*, the principal trade magazine of

A new can collection center in the heart of New York City.

the recycling industry: The subscription list jumped from 3,400 names to 11,000 in 1987–88 and has continued to grow each year since then.

But the economics of recycling are not always favorable to recyclers. Newsprint, for example, for years offered modest but steady profits to organizations and municipalities that sold used newspapers. By the end of the 1980s, however, the increase in recycling programs had changed that, causing the amount of recycled newsprint that was available to papermakers to grow far faster than their use of it. As a result, the value of recycled newsprint dropped, and many recycling programs languished.

Supporters of recycling say that the government will have to use financial incentives to keep recycling economically attractive. Such incentives might include loans at low rates of interest to recycling firms and tax breaks to manufacturers who increase their use of recycled materials. These and other incentives are already in place in some localities.

One factor often overlooked when the economics of recycling are examined is called "avoided costs," which refers to disposal costs that do not have to be paid by recyclers. Even if profits are low, recycling can save money by eliminating the need for costly disposal. For example, Pennsylvania authorities purchase paint and tar for the state's needs in 55-gallon barrels. Once the paint and tar are used, it costs $15 each to dispose of these barrels properly in a hazardous waste landfill. By selling them to recyclers at $3 each, the state earns $3 per barrel and saves $15 in avoided costs, for a total savings of $18 per barrel, or as much as $540,000 per year—not to mention the savings in landfill space.

The third major trend in recycling during the 1980s was a sudden spurt in the development of new kinds of technology, from lasers that can sort trash to degradable plastics. The most significant technological developments for the 1990s are expected to cluster around the problem of recycling plastics. Ever since their introduction, plastic products have been regarded as disposable, unlike paper, glass, and metal items, which have always been subject to at least a little recycling. Accordingly, the plastics industry paid scant attention to recycling until recently, and plastics recycling is still in its infancy. But each year the companies are spending a larger share of their budgets on research into new, more efficient ways to recycle plastics and on plastics recycling plants.

THE POWER OF GREEN
CONSUMING

For all the benefits it offers, recycling cannot solve all the world's waste disposal woes. This is why experts from both the EPA and scores of citizens' groups are looking toward source reduction as a vital step in controlling the trash crisis. Source reduction and recycling go hand in hand. If less trash is created, and more is recycled, then there will be a lot less left to dispose of. The EPA is counting on increased recycling to cut the waste stream by 25% by 1992, but it is also hoping that source reduction will account for a 25% drop in the waste stream, for an overall cut of 50%.

Source reduction attacks the cause of the trash problem, not its symptoms. It also recognizes that waste disposal does not stand alone but is part of a framework of interconnected environmental issues that includes resource and energy conservation, air and water pollution, toxic waste, and land use. Source reduction means that people must do more than dispose of trash in environmentally responsible ways. They must consider the waste stream that each item creates throughout its existence, as raw materials are mined or harvested, transported, manufactured into products, packaged, sold, used, and discarded.

Consumers who practice precycling not only save space in their trash cans and in the world's landfills but also accomplish other environmental goals: protecting the ozone layer of the atmosphere by not contributing to the use of chlorofluorocarbons that are found in aerosol cans and polystyrene foam; keeping forests alive as habitats for wildlife by cutting down on paper bags and reusing scrap paper; making limited petroleum resources last longer by becoming less dependent on plastic products; reducing water pollution from landfill leachate by using laundered cloth diapers instead of throwaway plastic ones; and reducing air pollution and acid rain by sending less trash to the local incinerator. The ultimate goal is to preserve a greater share of the planet's finite resources to be used by later generations.

Although governments have an important role to play in developing waste disposal policies, passing laws, and supporting the recycling industry with financial incentives, the success of both source reduction and recycling ultimately rests with consumers. Individuals can vote for elected officials who support source reduction and recycling, and they can also vote with their dollars. Consumers are increasingly ready to hit corporations where it really hurts them: in the pocketbook.

After the Exxon tanker *Valdez* ran aground and spilled oil in Prince William Sound, Alaska, a significant number of customers showed their displeasure with the company by canceling their Exxon credit cards. Many customers cut their cards to bits and mailed the pieces to the company's headquarters. When environmentalists publicized the fact that some fish-packing companies were using nets that captured and killed dolphins along with tuna, concerned consumers stopped buying canned tuna, and many of them wrote to Chicken of the Sea and other tuna packers urging them to adopt fishing methods that would not endanger dolphins. As a result, a number of fish-packing firms changed their netting practices, and cans of tuna began appearing in supermarkets with signs proclaiming them "Dolphin Safe."

The term *green consuming* has been coined to describe consumer habits that are based on an awareness of environmental issues. Green consumers practice precycling. They also try to buy products made by companies that comply with EPA regulations and show concern for environmental issues. Several guides that rate products and companies according to how well they meet certain environmental and social standards have been published in Great Britain and the United States. One of the best known is *Shopping for a Better World*, a guide to 1,300 brand name products from 138 companies. It was published by the Council on Economic Priorities in 1988 and rates products on the basis of their effect on the environment and other criteria. More than 350,000 copies had been sold by the end of 1989.

Corporations are reacting to the trend toward green consuming with a barrage of labels and claims intended to convince potential buyers that their products are environmentally sound. In many cases, these claims are meaningless or confusing because their use is not regulated by legal standards. The term *recyclable*, for example, appears on many products, leading some consumers to believe that these items are made from recycled materials, which is often not the case. Environmentalists and consumer advocates are calling for laws or federal standards to govern the use of labels like "organic" and "all-natural," which can often mean whatever a seller wants them to mean.

To help people who want to buy and use environmentally sound products, several nations have developed special symbols, called "ecomarks." West Germany introduced the first ecomark in 1978. Called the Blue Angel, it is now found on more than 3,500 products and indicates that those products are more environmentally sound than their competitors in the marketplace. In Canada, the Environmental Choice symbol—three doves whose tails form a maple leaf—is placed on products that meet government standards for pollution, resource recovery, toxicity, and recyclability. Japan has introduced an ecomark that shows a globe supported by two arms. The ecomark that is most used in the United States is the symbol for recycling, which consists of three arrows following each other around in a circle or triangle. This symbol can be found on recyclable goods, products made from recycled materials, bins used for separating recyclables, and recycling centers. In both industry and the environmental movement, there is growing demand for a single national or international ecomark and set of standards.

RECYCLING IN 2030

The May 1990 issue of *Natural History* magazine was a special issue devoted to recycling. It contained an article called "World Without End," in which authors Lester Brown, Christopher Flavin, and Sandra Postel showed what life could be like in the year 2030 if the recommendations of today's environmentalists became the way of the future.

In 2030, they predicted, waste reduction and recycling will have taken the place of trash collection and disposal. The throwaway habits of today's consumers will have been replaced by precycling and recycling. Government regulations will have slashed the amount of packaging that manufacturers and store owners can use. Shoppers will carry reusable canvas or string bags; with rare exceptions, paper and plastic bags will be museum relics. Societies will have voted to limit manufacturers and bottlers to a set of standard-size glass bottles and jars that can be steam-cleaned and used over and over again for everything from beer to fruit juice to vegetables. Human waste will be processed and returned to the land in the vegetable and fruit

At Union Square in New York City, these children participate in Earth Day activities by helping to clean up the square.

gardens and fish ponds that surround all cities and provide food for their inhabitants. All food and yard wastes will be composted, either by individual households or at communal composting centers that sell the humus they produce to the agriculture industry as an alternative to chemical fertilizers.

It is possible to add other predictions based on the suggestions of environmentalists. Households will pay for waste disposal based on the kind and amount of trash that each one generates. Those who fail to recycle or to sort waste properly will pay stiff fines, as will people who are caught littering. Every neighborhood will have a recycling center or a collection service or a drop-off point for recyclables. Industry, looking for environmentally sound ways to obtain raw materials, will operate many of them. Clothes, shoes, books, cars, bicycles, toys, and other consumer goods will be made almost entirely of recycled materials. New, easily recyclable plastics will have been developed; those that cannot be recycled will be used very little or not at all. High-technology incinerators will burn the residue of trash that cannot be recycled, producing energy in the process. In short, it will be as rare for something to be wasted in 2030 as it was in 1030. The young people of 2030 will read about the throwaway years of the 20th century and marvel that their parents and grandparents could have been so wasteful of the world's resources.

15 THINGS EVERYONE CAN DO NOW

Each of the following suggestions for controlling the waste stream has been recommended by at least two respected environmental spokespeople. Anyone who is interested in source reduction or recycling should be able to put at least one of these ideas into practice.

1. Learn about recycling in your community. If recycling is mandatory in your area, how does it work? If not, are there recyling centers or drop-off points nearby? What do they accept?

2. If you do not already recycle, try to make a habit of recycling at least one thing, such as aluminum cans or newspapers. Later you can include other recyclables.

3. Try reusables instead of disposables. For example, invest in a ballpoint pen with replaceable cartridges instead of a

throwaway; it will cost a little more, but you can use it over and over again.

4. Buy in large quantities to reduce the amount of packaging you bring home. Buy shampoo, for instance, in the largest bottle possible. If you need a smaller container for convenience, pour some of the shampoo into a small bottle that would otherwise be thrown away.

5. Cut down on junk mail. Americans receive 2 million tons of junk mail each year, and 44% of it goes into the trash unopened. Your family can reduce junk mail by up to 75% by writing to the Mail Preference Service of the Direct Marketing Association, 6 East 43 Street, New York, NY 10017, and asking to betaken off mass-mailing lists. You can send unwanted mail back to the sender by circling the return address and crossing out your name and address.

6. Precycle by buying products that come in glass, metal, or paper containers whenever possible.

7. Take your own string or canvas shopping bags or old grocery bags to the grocery store (but make sure that the store owner knows you are a thoughtful consumer and not a shoplifter).

8. Select fresh fruits and vegetables from display bins rather than those that come packaged in plastic and paper.

9. When eating at a fast-food restaurant, ask for a paper wrapper instead of a Styrofoam box for your food. You can also ask whether the restaurant has bins for sorting paper from plastic trash. Customer demand has caused a number of fast-food restaurants, including some McDonald's franchises, to begin sorting.

10. Do not throw away old clothes, books, toys, or furniture unless they are completely worn out and beyond further

The infamous Mobro *garbage barge. The Greenpeace organization has left a compelling message: Without recycling, societies will drown in their own waste.*

use. Instead, use the Yellow Pages or a local environmental organization to find a charity or a shelter for the homeless that will take usable items off your hands.

11. If your family subscribes to a lot of magazines, newspapers, and catalogs, suggest canceling all but the ones that always get read. Do not forget that you can browse through many papers and magazines at your library.

12. Buy products that are well made and will last. *Consumer Reports* rates hundreds of products, from CD players to sports equipment. You may decide it is better to spend a little more for a product that will last longer or has a good repair warranty.

13. Support companies that sell recycled products. Most recycled products on their labels will say "100% Recycled," "Made from Recycled Paper," or something similar. Start with recycled writing paper and greeting cards, which are easy to find.

14. If you drive, keep your car's tires properly inflated and balanced. This makes your tires last longer and keeps them out of the landfills. It also saves energy by making your engine run up to 5% more efficiently.

15. Wipe out excess packaging. If you are choosing between two similar products, choose the one with less packaging (that is, the one in the smaller box or with fewer layers of material around it). Eventually, manufacturers will get the message. Write to the manufacturers of your three favorite products, telling them that you are an environmentally concerned consumer who hopes they are looking for ways to eliminate unneeded packaging.

Books and organizations that can provide more information about recycling and related environmental issues are listed in the back of this book.

APPENDIX: FOR MORE INFORMATION

Environmental Organizations

Environmental Action Foundation
1525 New Hampshire Avenue NW
Washington, DC 20036
(202) 745-4879

Environmental Defense Fund
257 Park Avenue South
New York, NY 10010
(212) 505-2100

Everest Environmental Expedition (E3)
3730 Wind Dance Lane
Colorado Springs, CO 80906

Greenpeace USA
1436 U Street NW
Washington, DC 20009
(202) 462-1177

INFORM
381 Park Avenue South
New York, NY 10016
(212) 689-4040

Institute for Local Self-Reliance
2425 18th Street NW
Washington, DC 20009
(202) 232-4108

National Resources Defense Council
40 West 20th Street
New York, NY 10011
(212) 727-2700

Renew America
1400 16th Street NW
Suite 710
Washington, DC 20036
(202) 232-2252

Work on Waste (WOW)
82 Judson Street
Canton, NY 13617
(315) 379-9200

Worldwatch Institute
1776 Massachusetts Avenue NW
Washington, DC 20036
(202) 452-1999

Government Agencies

Environmental Protection Agency (EPA)
401 M Street SW
Washington, DC 20460
(202) 382-2080

Recycling Industry Organizations

Aluminum Recycling Association
900 17th Street NW
Washington, DC 20006
(202) 785-5100

Institute of Scrap Recycling
   Industries, Inc.
1627 K Street NW
Washington, DC 20006-1704

National Recycling Coalition
1730 Rhode Island Avenue NW
Washington, DC 20007
(202) 625-6406

National Solid Waste
   Management Association
1730 Rhode Island Avenue NW
Washington, DC 20036
(202) 659-4613

Society of the Plastics Industry
1275 K Street NW
Suite 400
Washington, DC 20005
(202) 371-5200

FURTHER READING

Caplan, Ruth, and Environmental Action. *Our Earth, Ourselves.* New York: Bantam Books, 1990.

Chandler, William. *Materials Recycling: The Virtue of Necessity.* Washington, DC: Worldwatch Institute, 1983.

Council on Economic Priorities. *Shopping for a Better World.* New York: Council on Economic Priorities, 1988.

Earthworks Group. *50 Simple Things Kids Can Do to Save the Earth.* New York: Andrews & McMeel, 1990.

————. *50 Simple Things You Can Do to Save the Earth.* Berkeley, CA: Earthworks Press, 1989.

Elkington, John, Julia Hailes, and Joel Makower. *The Green Consumer.* New York: Penguin Books, 1990.

Environmental Defense Fund. *Coming Full Circle: Successful Recycling Today.* New York: Environmental Defense Fund, 1988.

Environmental Protection Agency. *Recycling Works: State and Local Solutions to Solid Waste Management Problems.* Washington, DC: EPA Office of Solid Waste, 1989.

Goldstein, Jerome. *Recycling: How to Reuse Wastes in Home, Industry, and Society.* New York: Schocken Books, 1979.

Hahn, James, and Lynn Hahn. *Re-cycling: Re-using Our World's Solid Wastes.* New York: Watts, 1973.

Hassol, Susan, and Beth Richman. *Recycling: 101 Practical Tips for Home and Work.* Snowmass, CO: Windstar Foundation, 1989.

Hershkowitz, Allen, and Eugene Salerni. *Garbage Management in Japan: Leading the Way.* New York: INFORM, 1989.

Jabs, Carolyn. *Re/uses: 2133 Ways to Recycle and Reuse the Things You Ordinarily Throw Away.* New York: Crown, 1982.

Lipsett, Charles. *100 Years of Recycling: From Yankee Tincart Peddlers to Wall Street Scrap Giants.* New York: Atlas, 1974.

Naar, Jon. *Design for a Livable Planet: How You Can Help Clean Up the Environment.* New York: Harper & Row, 1990.

New Jersey Department of Environmental Protection. *Here Today, Here Tomorrow.* Trenton: New Jersey Department of Environmental Protection, 1989.

Pavoni, Joseph, and John Heer. *Handbook of Solid Waste Disposal: Materials and Energy Recovery.* New York: Van Nostrand Reinhold, 1975.

Pawley, Martin. *Building for Tomorrow: Putting Waste to Work.* San Francisco: Sierra Club Books, 1982.

Pollock, Cynthia. *Mining Urban Wastes: The Potential for Recycling.* Washington, DC: Worldwatch Institute, 1987.

Purcell, Arthur. *The Waste Watcher's Guide: A Citizen's Handbook for Conserving Energy and Resources.* New York: Anchor Books/Doubleday, 1980.

Rifkin, Jeremy, ed. *The Green Lifestyle Handbook: 1001 Ways You Can Heal the Earth.* New York: Holt, Rinehart & Winston, 1990.

Robinson, William, ed. *The Solid Waste Handbook: A Practical Guide.* New York: John Wiley, 1986.

Russell, Helen. *Earth: The Great Recycler.* Nashville: Nelson, 1976.

Seymour, John, and Herbert Girardet. *Blueprint for a Green Planet: Your Practical Guide to Restoring the World's Environment.* New York: Prentice-Hall, 1987.

Steger, Will, and Jon Bowermaster. *Saving the Earth: A Citizen's Guide to Environmental Action.* New York: Knopf, 1990.

Underwood, Joanna, Allen Hershkowitz, and Maarten de Kadt. *Garbage: Practices, Problems, and Remedies.* New York: INFORM, 1988.

Wirka, Jeanne. *Wrapped in Plastic: The Environmental Case for Reducing Plastic Packaging.* Washington, DC: Environmental Action Foundation, 1990.

Periodicals

BioCycle: Journal of Waste Recycling, J. G. Press, 18 South Seventh Street, Emmaus, PA 18049.

Garbage: The Practical Journal for the Environment, P.O. Box 56520, Boulder, CO 80321.

P3: The Earth-based Magazine for Kids, P.O. Box 52, Montgomery, VT 05470.

Solid Waste Report, Business Publishers, Inc., 951 Pershing Drive, Silver Spring, MD 20912.

Waste Age and *Waste Alternatives,* National Solid Waste Management Association, 1730 New Hampshire Avenue NW, Washington, DC 20036.

GLOSSARY

acid gases
Released during the process of incineration, these gases—sulfur dioxide and hydrochloric acid are the most common—are thought to contribute to the problem of acid rain and are often cited as a drawback of incineration as a method of disposing excess trash.

bauxite
The primary source for aluminum, this ore is increasingly expensive to mine and transport.

benzene
A toxic, flammable liquid used in the manufacture of polystyrene, or Styrofoam. Benzene has been proven to cause cancer.

biodegradable
Able to be broken down into constituent elements by natural biological processes such as decay and absorbed into the environment as food, elemental compounds, or other reusable raw materials.

chlorofluorocarbons
Known as CFCs, these useful but environmentally costly gases are thought to be the primary cause of the degradation of the earth's protective ozone layer. They play an important role in the manufacture of polystyrene foam.

compost
Organic material—food wastes, leaves, grass clippings, and excrement—that is allowed to decay in a controlled environment such as a pit or heap and that can be used as fertilizer.

cullet
Broken glass that is mixed with the raw materials of glassmaking to make the process quicker and more energy efficient.

dioxin
A toxic substance, known to cause cancer in animals, that is produced when materials containing chlorine (such as white paper and many plastics) are burned.

fly ash
Part of the residue left after trash is burned in an incinerator. About 10% of the ash produced during a typical incineration is fly ash, which is extremely fine and can be carried on the air. Fly ash, which can contain harmful or toxic substances such as dioxins, lead, cadmium, and mercury, is generally disposed of in landfills.

green belts
Areas of small farms that surround cities and absorb the organic waste produced by the cities as fertilizer. Long a fixture of Chinese and Indian food production, green belts are likely to play an important role in the industrial world's attempts to reduce waste.

landfill
A method of trash or garbage disposal in which the waste is supposed to be buried or sandwiched between layers of earth; although in many landfills, coverage of the trash is inadequate. Landfills are generally sited in marshy or low-lying land, which is gradually built up as the landfills are filled.

leach
The process by which solid substances are absorbed or carried along by liquids that trickle through them. The liquid formed by this process is called leachate.

mass burn facility
An incinerator that burns unsorted waste—including organic and inorganic material, food, paper, bottles, cans, clothing, and so on.

midden
A pit in which trash or garbage is buried. Middens are usually used in connection with organic garbage, such as kitchen wastes.

MSW
Municipal solid wastes; the aggregation of trash formed when waste is collected by a township or city from individual homes and businesses.

NIMBY
From "not in my back yard," NIMBY is used to describe the attitude of individuals, environmental organizations, and citizens' groups

that oppose the construction of new landfills, incinerators, nuclear power plants, and toxic waste disposal sites.

precycle
A term used by environmentalists to describe the consumer's responsibility before purchasing a product. A consumer should ask such such questions as: What does this item contain? How was it made? Is it reusable? How can it be recycled? Does it have unnecessary packaging?

recovery rate
The percentage of a resource that is recycled. For example, in the United States in 1990, the recovery rate for newsprint was about 30%.

scrubbers
An important part of state-of-the-art incinerator technology, these devices are supposed to remove the air pollutants created when trash is burned. Their effectiveness is still widely debated.

source reduction
Sometimes called preventive recycling—or simply making less trash. Source reduction lowers the amount of waste produced through the adoption of more environmentally responsible methods of manufacturing, packaging, and purchasing goods.

source separation
Sorting trash—for example, into separate containers for bottles, cans, and newspapers—where it is produced, as in a household or community collection center, rather than at a landfill or commercial recycling facility. Source separation reduces the cost of recycling.

stuff
The fully treated mixture of virgin and recycled materials that is ready to be rolled, dried, and cut into finished paper.

virgin material
Raw material for manufacturing that has never been recycled; straight from nature.

waste stream
The total output of trash, garbage, and discarded materials produced by a community or, on a larger scale, by a society or population.

Index

Air pollution, 19–23, 32, 37–38,
    55, 60–62, 66, 76, 86, 89,
    95–97, 104, 107–8
Aluminum, 14, 30, 39, 47, 52, 57,
    60–63, 65–66, 82, 86–87, 89,
    104, 112
American Newspaper Publishers
    Association, 49
Ash, 15, 21–24, 28, 32, 37, 52, 91,
    93, 95
Athens, Greece, 15–16
Automobile tires, 14, 78–79, 115

Bauxite, 62, 66
Biocycle, 82
Biodegradable, 28, 54, 75–76
Birkbeck, David, 88
Brown, Lester, 110

Canada, 86, 88, 109–10
Canadian Ministry of the
    Environment, 87
Center for the Biology of Natural
    Systems, 81
Chemical waste, 19, 76, 91, 93, 95
China, 41–42, 52
Chlorofluorocarbons (CFCs), 76,
    107
Coming Full Circle, 86–88
Composting, 51–52, 83, 86, 95,
    111
Connett, Paul, 90
Consumer Reports, 114

Council on Economic Priorities,
    109
Cullet, 58

Design for a Livable Planet (Naar),
    60
Disposable products, 14, 17, 18,
    36, 69, 71, 75–76, 93–94,
    96–97, 106, 108, 112–13

Earth Day, 37–39
EarthWorks Group, 60–61
Ecomarks, 109–10
Egypt, 17, 41
Energy conservation, 20, 49, 55,
    60–61, 66–67, 78, 90, 96, 107
England, 30, 109
Environmental Action Foundation,
    60, 79
Environmental Defense Fund, 87
Environmental Protection Agency
    (EPA), 18–20, 39, 55, 66, 73,
    81, 85, 95, 107, 109

Flavin, Christopher, 110
Florida, 13, 23, 85
Fossil fuels, 30, 66, 70, 73, 107

Glass, 17, 19, 25, 30, 34, 36,
    38–39, 47, 57–58, 60–61, 69,
    73, 85–86, 88–90, 97, 101,
    104, 106, 110, 113
Glass Packaging Institute, 60

Glenn, Jim, 82
Global warming, 55, 76, 107
Green Consuming, 107–10, 112–15
Greenpeace, 24–25, 27
Gutenberg, Johannes, 42

Hendry, George, 28
Hershkowitz, Allen, 95
High Bridge, New Jersey, 85–86
High-density polyethylene (HDPE), 71
High-technology resource recovery units (HTRRs). *See* Incinerators

Incinerators, 16, 19–24, 27, 33, 35–38, 47–48, 54–55, 82, 89, 91, 94–95, 104, 108, 112
  energy production, 20, 36, 86, 112
India, 17, 52
Islip, New York, 23–25

Japan, 14, 49, 90, 95, 110

Kian Sea/Pelicano, 91

Landfills, 13–15, 19–20, 22–25, 27, 33, 35, 37–38, 47–48, 51, 54, 61, 65, 75–76, 78, 82, 88–89, 91, 94–95, 104, 106, 108, 115
Lasers, 90, 106
Leachate, 14, 19, 22–23, 75, 95, 108
Leominster, Massachusetts, 77
Lignin, 45
London, England, 16

Louisiana, 23, 85
Low-density polyethylene (LDPE), 71

McDonald's, 77, 113
Maine, 13, 60
Manila, Philippines, 13
Maryland, 20, 83
Mass regional facilities (MRFs), 82
Medical waste, 19, 93
Metal, 17–18, 25, 34, 36, 38–39, 57–58, 60–62, 69, 73, 85, 89–90, 94, 106, 113
Methane, 19
Mexico City, Mexico, 17, 29
Middens, 15
Mobro, 23–24, 27
Mount Everest, 14–15
Municipal solid wastes (MSW). See Trash

National Consumers League, 61
National Resources Defense Council, 95
National Solid Waste Management Association, 81
Natural History, 28, 110
New Jersey, 20, 83, 104
New Mexico, 20
New York, 49–50, 60, 83
New York, New York, 13–14, 23–24, 29, 61
New York Times, 55
North Carolina, 23, 83
North Stonington, Connecticut, 88–89

Ohio, 20, 85
Ontario, Canada, 86–88

Oregon, 60, 83
Organic waste, 15, 18–19, 28, 30,
    33–34, 41, 51–52, 54, 75, 86,
    89, 110–11
Packaging, 18, 54, 69, 71–73, 83,
    97–99, 107, 113, 115
Paper, 14, 17–18, 25, 30, 33–34,
    36, 38–39, 41–45, 47–51,
    54–55, 57–58, 69, 73, 86,
    88–90, 97, 104–7, 113
    newsprint, 30, 41, 43, 45,
        48–49, 54–55, 86, 88–89,
        102, 105, 112, 114

Pennsylvania, 83, 106
Philadelphia, Pennsylvania, 20, 91
Plastic, 19, 30, 34, 39, 52, 58,
    69–73, 76, 77, 79, 86, 93–94,
    97, 104, 107, 112
    degradable, 74–76, 106
    soda bottles, 14, 30, 60, 71–72
    types, 69–72, 74–75
Pollack, Cynthia, 36
Polyethylene terephthalate (PET),
    71–72, 74, 79, 86
Polypropylene (PP), 71
Polystyrene (PS), 18, 72, 74–79,
    102, 113
Polyvinyl chloride (PVC), 71
Postel, Sandra, 110
Precycling, 83, 95–99, 108, 110,
    112–113
Prince William Sound, Alaska, 108

Rags, 34, 41–42, 45
Recovery rate, 19, 48–49, 60–61,
    63, 65, 71, 73, 78–79, 89–90,
    97
Recycling, 17, 19, 25, 27–28,
    31–32, 36–39, 42, 44, 47–48,
    51–52, 55, 57, 60–63, 65–67,
    69–73, 76–78, 81–83, 85–91,
    93, 95, 99, 101–6, 109–13.
    See also individual material
    economics, 25, 47–50, 60,
        62–63, 65, 88–89, 102–3,
        105–6, 115
    enforcing, 85–86, 89, 111
    fast facts, 54–55, 60–61,
        65–66, 79
    goals, 81–82, 85, 102, 107
    historical view, 34–35, 101
    industry support, 62–63, 65,
        73–74, 77, 79, 87, 97, 104,
        106, 112
    international, 90, 104
    laws, 25, 39, 58, 60, 71,
        82–83, 85–89, 102–3
    new uses for recycled
        materials, 31, 39, 48–49, 70,
        72, 77–79, 104
    reuse of material, 16, 30,
        42–45, 47–49, 55, 58,
        61–62, 65–67, 73, 79, 97,
        101–2, 107, 112, 115
    social concerns, 65, 86, 113
    sorting, 17, 47, 58, 71–72, 82,
        86, 89–90
Recycling Today, 104–5
Resins, 70–72, 76
Rubber, 19, 78–79

Saving the Earth: A Citizen's
    Guide to Environmental Action,
    18, 35, 101
Scrap dealers, 36, 58, 61, 65, 72,
    82, 88, 101, 104
Seattle, Washington, 88–90
Sewage, 33–34, 52, 91, 110–11
Shopping for a Better World, 109

Source reduction, 83, 95–99, 107, 112
Staten Island, New York, 13
Steel, 62, 65–67
Steel Can Recycling Institute, 65
Styrofoam. See *Polystyrene*
Suffolk County, New York, 73–74

Third World dumping, 91, 104
Trash, 14–17, 19, 29–30, 33–34, 36, 65, 67, 76, 85, 88–90, 93–94, 112. *See also* Waste stream
   composition, 14, 18–19, 32–33, 39, 41, 51, 54, 57, 61, 66, 69, 78, 81, 97, 113
   sorting, 17, 33–34, 36–37, 39, 58, 82, 85–86, 88–90, 95, 106, 111, 113
Trash pickers, 13, 16–17
Tokyo, Japan, 29

U.S. Department of Agriculture, 97

Valdez, 108
Virginia, 20, 85

Waste disposal services, 16, 33, 36, 85–86, 89
Waste stream, 32–34, 36, 39, 41, 51, 54, 57, 61, 66, 69, 73, 81, 83, 90, 93, 99, 101–2, 107
Water pollution, 14, 23, 37–38, 60–61, 66, 96–97, 104, 107–8
West Germany, 14, 90, 95, 109
Wildlife preservation, 37, 76, 86, 107–8
Wood, 14, 19, 34, 36, 42, 45
Work on Waste, 90
World Trade Center, 61
World War II, 17, 36, 38, 42
Worldwatch Institute, 36

PICTURE CREDITS

ABOUT THE AUTHOR

REBECCA STEFOFF is a Philadelphia-based freelance writer and editor who has published more than 40 nonfiction books for young adults. Many of her books deal with geography and exploration, and she takes an active interest in environmental issues and global ecology. She has also served as the editorial director of Chelsea House's *Places and Peoples of the World* and *Let's Discover Canada* series. Stefoff received her M.A. and Ph.D. degrees in English from the University of Pennsylvania, where she taught for three years.

ABOUT THE EDITOR

RUSSELL E. TRAIN, currently chairman of the board of directors of the World Wildlife Fund and The Conservation Foundation, has had a long and distinguished career of government service under three presidents. In 1957 President Eisenhower appointed him a judge of the United States Tax Court. He served Lyndon Johnson on the National Water Commission. Under Richard Nixon he became under secretary of the Interior and, in 1970, first chairman of the Council on Environmental Quality. From 1973 to 1977 he served as administrator of the Environmental Protection Agency. Train is also a trustee or director of the African Wildlife Foundation; the Alliance to Save Energy; the American Conservation Association; Citizens for Ocean Law; Clean Sites, Inc.; the Elizabeth Haub Foundation; the King Mahendra Trust for Nature Conservation (Nepal); Resources for the Future; the Rockefeller Brothers Fund; the Scientists' Institute for Public Information; the World Resources Institute; and Union Carbide and Applied Energy Services, Inc. Train is a graduate of Princeton and Columbia Universities, a veteran of World War II, and currently resides in the District of Columbia.